EFFECTIVE ECOLOGICAL MONITORING

David B. Lindenmayer and Gene E. Likens

CSIRO PUBLISHING

earthscan

publishing for a sustainable future

London • Washington, DC

National Library of Australia Cataloguing-in-Publication entry

Lindenmayer, David.

Effective ecological monitoring / David B. Lindenmayer ; Gene E. Likens.

9780643096837 (pbk.)

Includes index.
Bibliography.

Environmental monitoring.
Biodiversity conservation.
Environmental management.

Likens, Gene E., 1935–

363.7063

Library of Congress Cataloging-in-Publication Data has been applied for.

Published exclusively in Australia and New Zealand by

CSIRO PUBLISHING
150 Oxford Street (PO Box 1139)
Collingwood VIC 3066
Australia

Telephone: +61 3 9662 7666
Local call: 1300 788 000 (Australia only)
Fax: +61 3 9662 7555
Email: publishing.sales@csiro.au
Web site: www.publish.csiro.au

Published exclusively in all territories of the world excluding Australia and New Zealand by Earthscan, with
ISBN 978-1-84971-145-6 (paperback) and
ISBN 978-1-84971-144-9 (hardback).

Earthscan
Dunstan House
14a St Cross Street
London, ECIN 8XA, UK

Telephone: +44 (0)20 7841 1930
Fax: +44 (0)20 7242 1474
Email: earthinfo@earthscan.co.uk
Web site: www.earthscan.co.uk

Earthscan LLC, 1616 P Street, NW,
Washington, DC 20036, USA

Front cover images by: John Manger (top left), Gene Likens (bottom left), David Blair (middle and right)

Set in 10.5/13 Adobe Minion and Optima
Edited by Janet Walker
Cover and text design by James Kelly
Typeset by Desktop Concepts Pty Ltd, Melbourne
Index by Russell Brooks
Printed in Australia by Ligare

The book has been printed on paper certified by the Programme for the Endorsement of Forest Chain of Custody (PEFC). PEFC is committed to sustainable forest management through third party forest certification of responsibly managed forests.

CSIRO PUBLISHING publishes and distributes scientific, technical and health science books, magazines and journals from Australia to a worldwide audience and conducts these activities autonomously from the research activities of the Commonwealth Scientific and Industrial Research Organisation (CSIRO).

The views expressed in this publication are those of the author(s) and do not necessarily represent those of, and should not be attributed to, the publisher or CSIRO.

PEFC

PEFC/21-31-17

CONTENTS

ACKNOWLEDGMENTS

We thank the Commonwealth Environment Research Facilities CERF) program of the Australian Federal Government for financial support and encouragement.

DBL has gained important perspectives from long-term studies and monitoring projects in several parts of south-eastern Australia. These have been supported by several organisations, particularly the Victorian Department of Sustainability and Environment, Parks Victoria, and the recently terminated Land and Water Australia. These studies could not have taken placed without the expert professional statistical advice and support of Ross Cunningham, Jeff Wood and Alan Welsh. Nor could they have continued without the dedicated support of key field staff including Matthew Pope, Ryan Incoll, Chris MacGregor, Mason Crane, Damian Michael, Rebecca Montague-Drake and Lachlan McBurney.

GEL has worked on the Hubbard Brook Ecosystem Study since 1962. The Hubbard Brook Ecosystem Study was initiated in 1963 with colleagues, F Herbert Bormann, Robert S Pierce and Noye M Johnson; throughout the years, numerous other colleagues, students and technicians have contributed extensively to this study. John S Eaton, Donald C Buso and Phyllis C Likens, three long-term support staff, contributed hugely to my part of the Hubbard Brook Ecosystem Study. Long-term financial support for these studies was provided by The National Science Foundation and The Andrew W Mellon Foundation. Additional support to GEL in the writing of this book was provided by The Australian National University, CERF, the Cary Institute of Ecosystem Studies and the National Science Foundation through the Hubbard Brook Long-Term Ecological Research and Long-Term Research in Environmental Biology programs. The Hubbard Brook Experimental Forest is operated and maintained by the US Forest Service, Newtown Square, Pennsylvania.

Phyllis C Likens, Rachel Muntz, Merridee Bailey and Marjorie Lindenmayer provided outstanding technical assistance and logistical support. Donald C Buso, Charles Krebs and Rachel Muntz read and commented on the entire text. Others provided help to specific parts: Thomas J Butler, Daniel Conley, Jerry Franklin, Wellington B (Buddy) Huffaker, Paul Huth, Rick Linthurst, Jim Nichols, Amy Schuler and Lynn Sticker. Alan Covich provided significant logistical advice for one of our extended writing sessions.

Boxes for the text were written by Charles Krebs and John Pastor. In addition, Penny Olsen provided an update on her heroic efforts to recover the Norfolk Island boobook owl.

We drew heavily in this book on the paper 'Adaptive Monitoring', published in *Trends in Ecology and Evolution* (Lindenmayer and Likens 2009). The order of authorship of this book was determined by a virtual 'flip-of-the-coin', as we both contributed more or less equally to the intellectual development and writing of this book.

We thank a series of anonymous reviewers for thoughtful comments on earlier versions of the book.

John Manger from CSIRO Publishing helped shape our manuscript into a book.

David B Lindenmayer and Gene E Likens
August 2009

PREFACE

'It always seems easier to raise funds for the acquisition of a new painting than it does for the air-conditioning or conservation of the works you have...'

Max Bourke (former CEO of the Australia Council for the Arts)

So too it is with monitoring. It is always regarded as a luxury – the last thing to be funded, the first to be cut and when it is done, it is often done poorly or filed away and not used. Yet, monitoring is critical to the maintenance of the life support systems on which we depend.

'Happy families are all alike, each unhappy family is unhappy in its own way'

Opening sentence from Anna Karenina *by Leo Tolstoy*

So too it is with monitoring. Successful monitoring programs have some common characteristics, but unsuccessful ones fail for a wide variety of reasons.

Lessons from paintings and families inspire our overarching objectives, which are to demonstrate the importance of long-term ecological monitoring programs and present a diagnosis of the features of good and successful ones and the problems that beset poor or failed monitoring programs. We then build on these insights and present a new paradigm – Adaptive Monitoring – that collects together the key characteristics of successful long-term monitoring programs in a logical and coherent framework. Our goal in developing this framework is to see major improvements in the quality, effectiveness and number of long-term ecological studies and monitoring programs; improvements that ultimately will be essential to the maintenance of life on Earth.

Because improving monitoring programs is such a fundamentally important task, our audience for this book is wide; it is aimed at not only other researchers but also resource managers and environmental policy-makers. It is also intended to be useful for educated lay people and citizen scientists with an interest in monitoring programs aimed at improving the environment. Nevertheless, we have written the book in a scholarly style with citations and cross-references to other material so that readers can access related work by other workers.

THE STRUCTURE OF THIS BOOK

This book is about a framework and underlying philosophy for effective ecological monitoring. It is not a manual of field techniques – whether to do point-interval counts of transects for monitoring birds or which equipment is needed to track changes in airshed quality.

Our book comprises five short chapters. Readers may wish to go to particular chapters or even read the chapters in random order. The summary and set of references at the end of each chapter are designed to give the reader both a quick overview and an opportunity to pursue particular topics in greater detail. In Chapter 1 we define three broad kinds of monitoring – curiosity-driven or passive monitoring, mandated monitoring and question-driven monitoring. We then outline some of the ecological values that can be generated from long-term datasets. We conclude Chapter 1 by discussing the poor record of long-term ecological monitoring programs as the primary motivation for writing this book. In Chapter 2 we discuss some of the reasons we believe many monitoring programs are of problematic quality and often fail. We then discuss some of the features of good monitoring programs in Chapter 3. Based on that discussion, we present our Adaptive Monitoring framework that incorporates many of the key features and ingredients that should characterise good and effective long-term monitoring programs. In Chapter 4, we present case studies of what we believe to be some good and problematic long-term ecological monitoring programs to illustrate the salient points in the previous two chapters. We are acutely aware that this is our considered opinion and that some readers will be offended by the content of Chapter 4, and we have ventured into this territory with trepidation. Nevertheless, we have written this book in the spirit of constructive criticism in the hope that the problems we identify might be avoided in new monitoring programs or rectified in existing ones. It seems to us that constructive criticism lies at the heart of good science, our emphasis being on 'constructive'. The final chapter, Chapter 5, not only summarises the main points of our book, but it offers some thoughts about why and how many more long-term monitoring programs might be instigated and how existing ones can be maintained and improved.

CAVEATS

This book is not intended to be an exhaustive treatment of the vast amount of literature on monitoring, but adequate references are given to guide the reader to the extensive sources. The book is relatively short, drawing on our personal experiences and perspectives as to what does and does not work in long-term ecological research and monitoring.

Our discussions are based on our respective expertise in long-term population studies and biodiversity monitoring (David B Lindenmayer, DBL) and long-term ecosystem and biogeochemical studies and environmental monitoring (Gene E Likens, GEL). We have targeted terrestrial and aquatic ecosystems. However, we believe that the general principles we outline are also relevant to marine ecosystems.

We have selected case studies to provide a range of long-term monitoring programs. However, we readily acknowledge that this book contains a bias to our own work. We also admit to a bias toward the science of long-term monitoring rather than strictly a policy perspective on this topic. This bias arose because we are both scientists and not policy-makers, policy implementers or resource managers. Nevertheless, we readily acknowledge (in Chapter 3) that partnerships among people with different roles and sets of skills are one of the fundamental ingredients of successful monitoring programs.

We have sought to focus more philosophically and conceptually on monitoring programs, and we do not make specific recommendations or give precise 'recipes' about 'how to do monitoring'. We do not present a detailed review of field methods to guide monitoring programs – there is a truly enormous amount of literature on methods that is readily accessible to those initiating new work or revising existing programs. We believe that a monitoring program generally needs to be tailored to a particular question or site. Also, we do not examine the equally extensive literature on statistical and analytical methods and experimental designs for monitoring programs.

Finally, we have endeavoured to present our opinions without religious-like 'fundagelical' fervour. We believe that too much of science is characterised by the attitude that 'my way is right and yours is wrong'. As we point out in Chapter 5, there will be occasions where the main 'rules' we propose to guide monitoring programs will be breached and yet valuable outcomes are still produced.

David B Lindenmayer and Gene E Likens
August 2009

Chapter 1

Introduction

Organisms, including humans, depend upon the integrity of ecosystems for their well-being and survival. High-quality ecological information collected over long periods provides valuable insights into changes in ecosystem structure, ecological processes and the services ecosystems provide. Without this information, we would have no knowledge about the changing status of the life support system of the planet. We consider such information, collected conscientiously and continuously for at least 10 years, and then analysed, to be long-term monitoring.

We see the broad area of monitoring falling into three types:

- *Curiosity-driven or passive monitoring.* This type is monitoring devoid of specified questions and with little or no purpose other than curiosity and no underlying experimental design. It may be done out of inquisitiveness, but has limited usefulness in addressing environmental problems or in discovering how the world works because: (**1**) it is not hypothesis-driven, (**2**) it lacks management interventions or different experimental treatments, which facilitate scientific understanding about such things like ecosystem responses to natural or human disturbance. Curiosity-driven or passive monitoring could be purely mindless or it could be based on other motivations (see Chapter 4).
- *Mandated monitoring.* This is monitoring for which environmental data must be gathered as a stipulated requirement of government legislation or a political directive. For example, monitoring of weather or river flow funded by governments and conducted by

government agencies would be mandated monitoring. Rigid quality assurance/quality control (QA/QC) protocols are usually strictly mandated in this type of monitoring. Mandated monitoring is driven by the potential to answer broad and often practical questions. These questions almost always are posed *post-hoc* of some environmental problem and are not derived from a conceptual model. Mandated monitoring does not attempt to identify or understand the mechanism influencing a change in an ecosystem or an entity. Rather, the focus is usually to identify trends in a given entity (e.g. whether environmental conditions are getting 'better or worse').

• *Question-driven monitoring*. This type of monitoring is guided by a conceptual model of an ecosystem or some other entity (e.g. a population of organisms), and guided by a rigorous experimental design. The use of a conceptual model will typically result in *a priori* predictions that are then tested as part of the monitoring program. This kind of monitoring might be undertaken by a single investigator or it might fall under a program like the US Long-Term Ecological Research network. In question-driven monitoring, mechanisms can be discovered whereby prospective scenarios of trends can be calculated and modelled (see Chapters 3 and 4). Often such learning is informed by strongly contrasting management interventions (Carpenter *et al.* 1995) and in statistical parlance such studies might be best termed 'longitudinal studies with interventions' (e.g. Lindenmayer *et al.* 2008). This approach can lead to robust predictive capacity and enable an investigator to pose new questions – an advantageous part of the new Adaptive Monitoring paradigm that we outline in Chapter 3 of this book. This predictive capacity can be of immense value for ecologists, resource managers and decision makers. In contrast, in curiosity-driven or passive monitoring, and to a lesser extent mandated monitoring, the predictive and prospective capability of monitoring can be limited (e.g. simply extending trend lines).

Obviously, there can be overlap between broad categories of monitoring. For example, a rigorous statistical framework can characterise both mandated and question-driven monitoring. There can be advantages and disadvantages of mandated monitoring programs and question-driven research and monitoring. As we discuss below, mandated monitoring is often coarse-scale, leading to assessments of resource condition, but providing limited understanding of ecological mechanisms giving rise to that condition. Question-driven monitoring is often the converse. It is finer scaled and often process-based, but it is very difficult to make valid spatial

---

BOX 1.1   WHAT IS NOT LONG-TERM MONITORING

Although one can easily do runs from a simulation model and make projections for thousands of years into the future, we do not consider simulation modelling *per se* to be long-term work. Although they can provide long-term perspectives, we also do not consider studies that substitute space-for-time (e.g. snapshot investigations (Diamond 1986) or retrospective investigations (Likens 1989) to be long-term work *per se*. We also do not consider haphazard revisits to a site after a prolonged absence to be programs of long-term research or monitoring (e.g. Currie and Parry 1999; Smith *et al.* 2007). Contrary to widely held beliefs in some organisations, we also do not believe that simply measuring something in the environment constitutes monitoring. Rather, as we outline in the following chapters, monitoring needs questions, an experimental design, a conceptual framework, and data integrity through repeatable application of appropriate field protocols.

We acknowledge there are many nuances to discussions about what constitutes 'long-term' in ecological research and monitoring. The review by Strayer *et al.* (1986) is instructive. They note that some workers consider long-term studies to be those that continue beyond the generation time of dominant organisms in an ecosystem or sufficiently long to quantify the key processes, which structure the ecosystem under investigation. This definition would mean that studies of bacterial assemblages with very rapid generation times would be long-term investigations if they persisted for a year or even a month. Conversely, a 300-year study of stands of giant sequoia (*Sequoiadendron giganteum*) in which the dominant trees may live for over 1000 years would not qualify as a long-term study. These considerations are important because they emphasise the variable lifespan of different organisms, but they are not feasible to use for many ecosystem analyses. For the purposes of this book, we use a practical, operational definition and consider long-term as monitoring efforts that continue beyond 10 years.

---

extrapolations to larger scales (e.g. at the state, province or national level). Thus, in Chapter 5, we discuss the challenges posed by the integration of data, insights and management recommendations from these two broad kinds of monitoring programs.

SOME OF THE ECOLOGICAL VALUES AND USES OF LONG-TERM DATASETS

Countless scientific articles, books, management plans and other documents have been written about the need to do long-term monitoring (e.g.

Strayer *et al.* 1986; Likens 1989; Goldsmith 1991; Likens 1992; Spellerberg 1994; Thompson *et al.* 1998; Franklin *et al.* 1999; Wiersma 2004; Lovett *et al.* 2007; Krebs *et al.* 2008). As part of writing this book, a search of the ecological literature published between 1985 and late 2008 produced more than 4200 articles with the term 'monitoring' in the title or abstract. There are even entire journals directly or indirectly focused on long-term research and monitoring programs. *Environmental Monitoring and Assessment* and *Journal of Environmental Monitoring* are two examples.

In this vast literature, many ecologists and managers of natural resources have readily acknowledged the importance of long-term research, which normally incorporates monitoring, for improved understanding and management of complex systems. Long-term data are valuable for many reasons. For example, they are fundamentally important for:

- documenting and providing baselines against which change or extremes can be evaluated (e.g. climate change);
- evaluating ecological responses to disturbance, such as from experimental manipulations;
- detecting and evaluating changes in ecosystem structure and function, such as change in forest biomass accumulation or change in nutrient limitation of aquatic productivity;
- generating new and important questions about population, community and ecosystem dynamics;
- providing empirical data for testing ecological theory and models, and
- data mining when exploring new questions.

In the remainder of this section, we illustrate some of these values with a few brief examples.

Time until expression

Long-term monitoring is important because many ecological phenomena and ecological processes take a long time to manifest, often on much longer temporal scales than are typical of most ecological or environmental measurements (Smith *et al.* 2007). For example, in marine ecosystems, oceanographic cycles occur over decades and perhaps even centuries, making long-term monitoring programs critical, although such programs are extremely uncommon in places like deep-sea environments (which also happens to be the largest environment on Earth).

Long-term datasets such as those gathered through continuous monitoring can be pivotal to evidence-based environmental legislation (e.g.

BOX. 1.2   TIME TO EXPRESSION – LONG-TERM MONITORING AT LAKE WASHINGTON, SEATTLE, USA

Increasing inputs of nutrients from sewage and other sources were contributing to Lake Washington (Seattle, Washington, USA) becoming increasingly eutrophic, especially during the 1940s and 50s (Edmondson 1991). A noxious, blue-green alga (the cyanobacterium, *Oscillatoria rubescens*) was first noticed in the lake in 1955. Although the city began to divert raw sewage to treatment plants in 1926, increased numbers of people, increased urban development and forest clearing in the catchment by the 1950s and 1960s, had increased nutrient loading to the lake. A local newspaper, the Seattle Post-Intelligencer, even referred to Lake Washington as 'Lake Stinko' (Edmondson 1991) because of the increased eutrophication. In response, local municipalities passed a bond issue ('Metro') in 1958 to fund the construction of a 'diverter system' ringing the lake to direct sewage away from the lake and into nearby Puget Sound. The diversion began in 1964; the phosphorus content promptly decreased and the lake began to recover. Long-term research and monitoring commenced in 1955 by Professor WT (Tommy) Edmondson and colleagues (Figure 1.1). Their work included retrospective studies, natural history studies and monitoring (Edmondson 1974; Edmondson and Litt 1982; Edmondson 1991) and was instrumental in not only establishing the basis for this management intervention, but also for chronicling its success (Edmondson 1991). In 1965, Professor Edmondson presented a scientific paper at the International Association of Theoretical and Applied Limnology (SIL) Congress in Warsaw, Poland where he made the prediction that the clarity of the lake in 1971 would be better than 1950 summer values had been. Scientific colleagues were sceptical of such a rapid recovery, and Professor Edmondson and Professor K Wuhrmann (a prominent Swiss scientist) entered into a public wager as to when the lake would recover. Edmondson won this bet, presenting his data in a paper at the SIL Congress in the Soviet Union in 1971 to great applause from the audience (Edmondson 1972). A bottle of fine liquor was awarded to Edmondson by Wuhrmann at a subsequent meeting in Kiel, to acknowledge and highlight publicly this successful interaction between long-term research (science), monitoring and management. This is an excellent example of the value of long-term research and monitoring for the public good in protecting and managing natural ecosystems. Long-term studies and monitoring are maintained on Lake Washington (DE Schindler, pers.comm.), which continues to change. For example, in 1976 the lake surprisingly became even more transparent than observed before, which was due to the appearance of significant numbers of *Daphnia spp.*, a zooplantonic grazer of small algae, requiring changes (adaptive) in the monitoring regime.

Figure 1.1 Professor Edmondson at Lake Washington, Seattle. (Photo by Ben Benschneider, courtesy of the *Seattle Washington Times*)

laws to control air and water pollutants). Legislation regulating the release of pollutants like carbon dioxide or sulphur dioxide is typically implemented without a clear view of the time frame of the response. In the USA, the Clean Air Act Amendments of 1970 and 1990 mandated a reduction in particulate and sulphur dioxide emissions from industrial combustion of coal and oil to reduce the amount of air pollution and acid rain falling on eastern North America. Emissions of sulphur dioxide to the atmosphere are a major precursor in the formation of acid rain. No-one had expected that prolonged data collection would be required to test the effectiveness of this legislation. It required 18 years of continuous monitoring of precipitation chemistry in the Hubbard Brook Experimental Forest in New Hampshire before ecologists could determine that the acidity of precipitation had actually decreased (Figure 1.2) (Likens 1989; Likens 1992) in response to these federally mandated reductions in emissions. This result was badly needed by policy-makers dealing with the problem of acid rain, but it took a long time to obtain this ostensibly 'simple' result (Likens 1992).

Use in simulation modelling

Simulation modelling is an important part of ecology and environmental management. However, the best simulation modelling will typically be based on an understanding of ecosystem structure and function, ecological process, and the biotic assemblage or species targeted for study (Burgman *et al.* 1993). Long-term empirical data are often essential for simulation modelling studies (Burgman *et al.* 1993). As an example, long-term

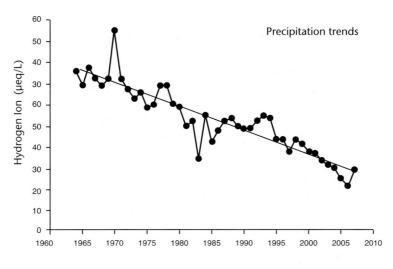

Figure 1.2 Changes in the volume-weighted annual acidity of precipitation from 1964 to 2009 at Hubbard Brook Experimental Forest, New Hampshire. (Modified and updated from Likens 1989)

ecological data were used in extensive population modelling studies of arboreal marsupials in the Central Highlands of Victoria in south-eastern Australia (Lindenmayer and McCarthy 2006). This work was motivated by a need to estimate the risk of extinction of iconic species such as the nationally endangered Leadbeater's possum (*Gymnobelidues leadbeateri*) (Lindenmayer and Possingham 1995; Lindenmayer and McCarthy 2006). Data used in the modelling included life history information (Smith 1984), information on long-term habitat dynamics based on known temporal relationships between vegetation structure and animal occurrence (Lindenmayer *et al.* 1994), long-term population trend information (Lindenmayer *et al.* 2003), and post-disturbance recovery processes in animal populations and forest composition and structure (Mackey *et al.* 2002). The results of modelling that were built upon these various kinds of data guided the development of mid-scale protected areas for the endangered species, Leadbeater's possum, within forests broadly designated for timber production (Lindenmayer and Possingham 1995). Long-term data underpinned not only an improvement to the reserve system, but also in the modelling *per se*, motivating a cycle of ongoing field data collection, test of simulation models, and continuous upgrading of simulation models (Lindenmayer and McCarthy 2006).

Tests of ecological theory

Empirical field data provide the only true test of ecological theory (Shrader-Frechette and McCoy 1993). This value has been demonstrated in virtually all ecosystems that have been studied worldwide. A classic example is the Kluane Boreal Forest Monitoring Project in northern Canada (see Box 1.3).

Vitousek and Reiners (1975) and Gorham *et al.* (1979) proposed a theory to explain the biogeochemical response of nitrogen to forest disturbance. They hypothesised that disturbed forest ecosystems will be 'leaky' (i.e. have limited retention) for nitrogen with large losses of nitrate in stream water. However, such systems would strongly retain nitrogen during aggradation stages of forest maturation. They also postulated that mature forests would be less retentive of nitrogen and become leaky again (e.g. increased nitrate lost in stream water). Long-term monitoring, combined with catchment-scale experimental manipulation of the Hubbard Brook Experimental Forest showed, however, that the current, 'mature' forest ecosystem is strongly retentive of nitrogen because nitrate concentrations in stream water are at the lowest concentration during the 46-year record (Likens 2004). Either the theory is inadequate or something else is happening, and this topic is currently the subject of intense monitoring and study (Bernal *et al.* 2010; Judd *et al.* 2010).

Surprises

Long-term monitoring can reveal significant ecological surprises of environmental and conservation consequence. An example is the population monitoring of the giant panda (*Ailuropoda melanoleuca*), a Chinese and global conservation icon. Populations of the species had been carefully monitored in the Wanglang Nature Reserve for many years and numbers were estimated to be just 27 individuals in 1998 (Zhan *et al.* 2006). However, in the mid-2000s, new survey methods were employed using molecular markers and to the great surprise of biologists, the population of the giant panda was estimated to be ~66 individuals or at least twice that thought in 1998 (Zhan *et al.* 2006). We further discuss the monitoring program for the giant panda in Chapter 2, particularly in regard to the use of standardised field protocols and relationships to the long-term maintenance of data integrity.

POOR RECORD OF LONG-TERM ECOLOGICAL MONITORING

Some in the scientific community have traditionally viewed monitoring as a management activity unrelated to scientific research (e.g. Hellawell 1991).

BOX 1.3 KLUANE BOREAL FOREST MONITORING PROJECT
Charles J. Krebs
University of British Columbia
Vancouver, Canada
http://www.zoology.ubc.ca/~krebs/kluane.html

In 1973, my students and I began studies in the boreal forest of the south-western Yukon, based out of the Arctic Institute's Kluane Lake Research Station, one of the few research stations in northern Canada. The original studies were centered on the small rodents, but it quickly became clear that the dominant herbivore in the ecosystem was the snowshoe hare. The research program was refocused on an attempt to understand the ecological mechanisms driving the nine- to 10-year cycle of snowshoe hares, a cycle that occurs across the boreal zone of Alaska and Canada. Tony Sinclair and Jamie Smith joined the Kluane Project in 1976 and we set up the first of a series of large-scale experiments to test hypotheses about the factors driving the hare cycle. From 1976 to 1984 we tested the food hypothesis by providing extra food to hares on four areas. The results were disappointing because adding food made no impact on the cyclic decline. By the early 1980s we had become convinced that predators were a major factor in this ecosystem, and we decided to expand the study to encompass the entire terrestrial food web from plant dynamics to predator changes. The research team expanded to eight faculty members from four Canadian universities, and from 1986 to 1996 we carried out a larger set of experiments manipulating the ecosystem bottom-up by adding fertiliser and hare food and top-down by predator exclusion with electric fences. The results have been summarised in a book (Krebs *et al.* 2001) and in over 265 publications.

By 1996 when the major funding ceased, we had to decide whether or not to stop the study. We decided to continue monitoring key elements in the food web: fungal and plant production, hare, squirrel, and the abundance of rodents and major predators. By 2009, we had gathered 36 years of monitoring data on rodents and hares in this ecosystem, 24 years of predator monitoring, and 12 to 15 years of monitoring the less studied components (fungi, ground berries). One result of this monitoring has led to unexpected insights since climate change became a major focus of research interest in northern Canada. For example, we have now developed a predictive model of how regional climate variables affect above-ground mushroom production (Krebs *et al.* 2008). Snowshoe hare cycles have shown a disturbing trend to lower peak population densities sequentially in the four cycles that we have monitored since 1973, a trend we are following with great interest. Red squirrels have adjusted their breeding season earlier in the spring as a response to climate change (Réale *et al.* 2003).

The monitoring has led to a range of hypotheses about ecosystem function in the plants and animals of the Yukon boreal forest. And while the major finding has been that for the terrestrial mammals this is largely a top-down system driven by the predators, rather than a bottom-up system driven by soil nutrients and plant production, as with most ecological systems, the devil is in the details of how the ecosystem components interact. The major question currently is to anticipate how this ecosystem will respond to climate change, and this question can now be addressed with a background set of quantitative data on the major species in this ecosystem.

This study could not have been done without a dedicated group of ecologists interested in understanding community dynamics in this ecosystem, an enthusiastic group of graduate students and technicians, and continued funding from the Natural Sciences and Engineering Research Council of Canada and two private foundations.

Moreover, monitoring has sometimes been considered a routine activity where data collected in this way do not merit significant consideration by managers ('mindless monitoring', i.e. an activity that is not 'science' or does not contribute to achieving goals or have an expected outcome) (Yoccoz *et al.* 2001; Nichols and Williams 2006). In contrast, we believe that well-conceived and well-executed monitoring is a fundamentally important component of scientific research. Good scientists lead with good questions and they develop good questions by: (1) using critical thinking; (2) building robust conceptual models of how ecosystems work to guide research; (3) testing 'true' policy questions (Walters 1986); (4) promoting open dialog between scientists and managers (Likens 1989; Lawton 2007; Likens *et al.* 2009), and (5) critically evaluating experimental manipulation, both designed and opportunistic.

BOX 1.4 NOT ALL ECOLOGICAL RESEARCH NEEDS TO BE LONG-TERM

Not all ecological studies need to be long-term. As an illustration, many kinds of studies in behavioural ecology can be completed relatively rapidly and will not necessarily benefit from repeated measurements over a prolonged period. For example, studies of the calling behaviour of birds will often be very informative when conducted as a 'snapshot investigation' at particular times of the day when all members of the bird assemblage are vocalising (Catchpole and Slater 1995).

Although there have been some highly successful long-term monitoring programs (e.g. Lund 1978; Goldman 1981; Lawes Agricultural Trust 1984; Likens and Bormann 1995; Schindler *et al.* 1985), there is a prolonged history of poorly planned and unfocused monitoring programs that are either ineffective or fail completely (see Orians 1986; Krebs 1991; Allen 1993; Norton 1996; Stankey *et al.* 2003; Legg and Nagy 2006).

In this book, we discuss some of the deficiencies in monitoring programs. Then, based upon our collective experience totalling 70 years in establishing natural resource and environmental monitoring programs, we discuss ways to resolve some of the problems underlying poorly planned and unfocused monitoring programs. As part of our discussion, we outline an Adaptive Monitoring framework. This framework is driven by tractable questions, a rigorous statistical design at the outset of the study, a human need to know about ecosystem change, and a plan to monitor a small number of things well rather than many entities badly. The framework allows a monitoring program to evolve and adapt iteratively as new information is obtained or new questions emerge, while maintaining the integrity of the core objectives of the initial program (Lindenmayer and Likens 2009).

WHY WE WROTE THIS BOOK

Why did we feel compelled to write yet something else on monitoring and add to an already enormous scientific and management literature? There were four key reasons for our decision:

1. Societal need

The first reason we wrote this book was to foster a renewed interest in, and an improvement of, ecological monitoring. We strongly believe it is now increasingly critical to do high-quality, question-driven, statistically designed monitoring, given the rapid increase in effects of climate change and the need to reverse the current, widespread environmental crisis. It could be argued (and we do) that given the increasing environmental degradation throughout the world, there never has been a more important time to establish good and effective monitoring networks.

2. Making sense of the vast monitoring literature

There is an immense and rapidly increasing body of literature on monitoring and monitoring-related topics. Much of it can be very confusing for scientists, policy-makers and resource managers alike. Although this book is short, we invested great effort in reading a very large amount of the literature on ecological monitoring and in doing so, attempted to alert readers to some distinct biases that often may not be particularly useful for many people proposing to initiate new monitoring programs.

First, much has been written about specific methods of monitoring a particular entity, but these will often be relevant only to that entity (e.g. a species or group of species) or to a given place; they will not be readily transferable to other entities or landscapes. Phrases like 'this should be useful for monitoring' or 'X should be monitored' appear repeatedly in the literature but without much discussion of why and in what circumstances.

A second bias in the monitoring literature is on generic lists of entities that are advocated as 'mandatory' to monitor and generic frameworks to guide the measurement of these entities. These lists and frameworks are often illustrated with a case study from a particular ecosystem, but the transferability of these approaches to other ecosystems can be problematic.

Third, much of the monitoring literature focuses on statistical methods and experimental design. While this information is valuable, much of it may not be relevant for addressing specific questions or problems that a particular monitoring program aims to address.

Fourth, much of the monitoring literature has discussed 'indicators' and contains claims that entity X or species Y is an 'indicator'. Often these claims are unsubstantiated. Where they are substantiated, the generality of the indicator function can be limited, either spatially, taxonomically or both, and this approach may not be helpful for those proposing to establish new monitoring programs.

3. Providing an overview of success and failure

A third key reason why we wrote this book was that the numbers of monitoring studies worldwide is now sufficient to allow us to identify what we believe makes an effective monitoring program. It is important to identify factors that contribute to success and failure so that the public perspectives of ecological monitoring are improved and bureaucrats do not lose patience with the scientific community and abandon funding investments in monitoring programs.

4. New perspectives

We believe we have identified some important new perspectives on monitoring programs that, to the best of our knowledge, have not previously been canvassed by others. One of these is the Adaptive Monitoring paradigm and the framework that accompanies it. Similarly, we have not found other treatments of the advantages and disadvantages of mandated monitoring programs and question-driven research and monitoring. Finally, we believe we have identified some confusion of scale and function among monitoring programs. As we outlined above (and discuss further in Chapter 5), mandated monitoring is often coarse-scale and focused on resource condition whereas question-driven monitoring is often sites-based and/or finer scaled, often with a focus on ecological processes. We believe these differences are often overlooked in the literature in an effort to develop an all encompassing, 'one-size-fits-all' framework. This generality can lead to arguments at cross-purposes, particularly about the relative merits of different approaches, frameworks, and methods.

REFERENCES

Allen RB (1993) An appraisal of monitoring studies in South Island tussock grasslands, New Zealand. *New Zealand Journal of Ecology* **17**, 61–63.

Bernal S, Hedin LO, Likens GE, Gerber S and Buso DC (2010) Complex response of the forest nitrogen cycle to climate change. *In preparation*.

Burgman MA, Ferson S and Akçakaya HR (1993) *Risk Assessment in Conservation Biology*. Chapman and Hall, New York, London.

Carpenter SR, Chisholm SW, Krebs CJ, Schindler DW and Wright RF (1995) Ecosystem experiments. *Science* **269**, 324–327.

Catchpole CK and Slater PJ (1995) *Bird Song. Biological Themes and Variations*. Cambridge University Press, Cambridge, UK.

Currie DR and Parry GD (1999) Changes to benthic communities over 20 years in Port Phillip Bay, Victoria. *Marine Pollution Bulletin* **38**, 36–43.

Diamond J (1986) Overview: laboratory experiments, field experiments and natural experiments. In *Community Ecology*. (Eds J Diamond and TJ Case) pp. 3–22. Harper and Row, New York.

Edmondson WT (1972) The present condition of Lake Washington. *Verhandlungen der Internationalen Vereinigung für Theoretische und Angewandte Limnologie* **18**, 284–291.

Edmondson WT (1974) Secondary production. *Mitteilungen der Internationalen Vereinigung für Theoretische und Angewandte Limnologie* **20**, 229–274.

Edmondson WT (1991) *The Uses of Ecology: Lake Washington and Beyond*. University of Washington Press, Seattle.

Edmondson WT and Litt AH (1982) Daphnia in Lake Washington. *Limnology and Oceanography* **27**, 272–293.

Franklin JF, Harmon ME and Swanson FJ (1999) Complementary roles of research and monitoring: lessons from the U.S. LTER Program and Tierra del Fuego. Paper presented to the Symposium. Paper presented at 'Toward a unified framework for inventorying and monitoring forest ecosystem resources', Guadalajara, Mexico, November 1998.

Goldman C (1981) Lake Tahoe: two decades of change in a nitrogen deficient oligotrophic lake. *Verhandlungen der Internationalen Vereinigung für Theoretische und Angewandte Limnologie* **21**, 45–70.

Goldsmith B (1991) *Monitoring for Conservation and Ecology*. Chapman and Hall, London.

Gorham E, Vitousek PM and Reiners WA (1979) The regulation of chemical budgets over the course of terrestrial ecosystem succession. *Annual Review of Ecology and Systematics* **10**, 53–84.

Hellawell JM (1991) Development of a rationale for monitoring. In *Monitoring for Conservation and Ecology*. (Ed. FB Goldsmith) pp. 1–14. Chapman and Hall, London.

Judd KE, Likens GE, Buso DC and Bailey A (2010) Minimal response in watershed nitrate export to severe soil frost raises questions about nutrient dynamics in the Hubbard Brook Experimental Forest. Submitted for publication.

Krebs CJ (1991) The experimental paradigm and long-term population studies. *Ibis* **133**, 2–8.

Krebs CJ, Boutin S and Boonstra R (Eds) (2001) *Ecosystem Dynamics of the Boreal Forest: the Kluane Project*. Oxford University Press, New York.

Krebs CJ, Carrier P, Boutin S, Boonstra R and Hofer EJ (2008) Mushroom crops in relation to weather in the southwestern Yukon. *Botany* **86**, 1497–1502.

Lawes Agricultural Trust (1984) *Rothamsted: The Classical Experiments*. Rothamsted Agricultural Experiment Station, Rothamsted, England.

Lawton JH (2007) Ecology, politics and policy. *Journal of Applied Ecololgy* **44**, 465–474.

Legg CJ and Nagy L (2006) Why most conservation monitoring is, but need not be, a waste of time. *Journal of Environmental Management* **78**, 194–199.

Likens GE (Ed.) (1985) *An Ecosystem Approach to Aquatic Ecology: Mirror Lake and its Environment*. Springer-Verlag, New York.

Likens GE (Ed.) (1989) *Long-term Studies in Ecology. Approaches and Alternatives*. Springer-Verlag, New York.

Likens GE (1992) *The Ecosystem Approach: Its Use and Abuse*. Ecology Institute, Oldendorf/Luhe, Germany.

Likens GE (2004) Some perspectives on long-term biogeochemical research from the Hubbard Brook Ecosystem Study. *Ecology* **85**, 2355–2362.

Likens GE and Bormann FH (1995) *Biogeochemistry of a Forested Ecosystem*. Second edition. Springer-Verlag, New York.

Likens GE, Walker K, Davies P, Brookes J, Olley J, Young W, Thoms M, Lake S, Gawne B, Davis J, Arthington A, Thompson R and Oliver R (2009) Ecosystem science:

toward a new paradigm for managing Australia's inland aquatic ecosystems. *Marine and Freshwater Research* **60**, 271–279.

Lindenmayer DB, Cunningham RB and Donnelly CF (1994) The conservation of arboreal marsupials in the montane ash forests of the Central Highlands of Victoria, south-eastern Australia. 6. The performance of statistical-models of the nest tree and habitat requirements of arboreal marsupials applied to new survey data. *Biological Conservation* **70**, 143–147.

Lindenmayer DB, Cunningham RB, MacGrego, C and Incoll RD (2003) A long-term monitoring study of the population dynamics of arboreal marsupials in the Central Highlands of Victoria. *Biological Conservation* **110**, 161–167.

Lindenmayer DB, Cunningham RB, McGregor C, Crane M, Michael D, Montague-Drake R, Fischer J, Felton A and Manning A (2008) The changing nature of bird populations in woodland remnants as a pine plantation emerges: results from a large-scale 'natural experiment' of landscape context effects. *Ecological Monographs* **78**, 567–590.

Lindenmayer DB and Likens GE (2009) Adaptive monitoring – a new paradigm for long-term research and monitoring. *Trends in Ecology and Evolution* **24**, 482–486.

Lindenmayer DB and McCarthy MA (2006) Evaluation of PVA models of arboreal marsupials. *Biodiversity and Conservation* **15**, 4079–4096.

Lindenmayer DB and Possingham HP (1995) *The Risk of Extinction: Ranking Management Options for Leadbeater's Possum*. Centre for Resource and Environmental Studies, Canberra.

Lovett GM, Burns DA, Driscoll CT, Jenkins JC, Mitchell MJ, Rustad L, Shanley JB, Likens GE and Haeuber R (2007) Who needs environmental monitoring? *Frontiers in Ecology and the Environment* **5**, 253–260.

Lund J (1978) Changes in the phytoplankton of an English lake, 1945–1977. *Hydrobiology Journal* **14**, 10–27.

Mackey B, Lindenmayer DB, Gill AM, McCarthy MA and Lindesay JA (2002) *Wildlife, Fire and Future Climate: A Forest Ecosystem Analysis*. CSIRO Publishing, Melbourne.

Nichols JD and Williams BK (2006) Monitoring for conservation. *Trends in Ecology and Evolution* **21**, 668–673.

Norton DA (1996) Monitoring biodiversity in New Zealand's terrestrial ecosystems. In *Papers from a Seminar Series on Biodiversity*. (Eds B McFadgen and S Simpson) pp. 19–41. Department of Conservation, Wellington, New Zealand.

Orians GH (1986) The place of science in environmental problem-solving. *Environment* **28**, 12–17, 38–41.

Réale D, McAdam AG, Boutin S and Berteaux D (2003) Genetic and plastic responses of a northern mammal to climate change. *Proceedings of the Royal Society of London, Series B* **270**, 591–596.

Schindler DW, Mills KH, Malley DF, Findlay DL, Shearer JA, Davies IJ, Turner MA, Linsey GA and Cruikshank DR (1985) Long-term ecosystem stress: the effects of years of experimental acidification on a small lake. *Science* **228**, 1395–1401.

Shrader-Frechette KS and McCoy ED (1993) *Method in Ecology: Strategies for Conservation*. Cambridge University Press, Cambridge.

Smith AP (1984) Demographic consequences of reproduction, dispersal and social interaction in a population of Leadbeater's Possum *Gymnobelideus leadbeateri*. In *Possums and Gliders*. (Eds AP Smith and ID Hume) pp. 359–373. Surrey Beatty & Sons, Sydney.

Smith TB, Purcell J and Barino JF (2007) The rocky intertidal biota of the Florida Keys: fifty-two years of change after Stephenson and Stephenson (1950). *Bulletin of Marine Science* **80**, 1–19.

Spellerberg IF (1994) *Monitoring Ecological Change*. Second edition. Cambridge University Press, Cambridge.

Stankey GH, Bormann BT, Ryan C, Shindler B, Sturtevant V, Clark RN and Philpot C (2003) Adaptive management and the Northwest Forest Plan – rhetoric and reality. *Journal of Forestry* **101**, 40–46.

Strayer DL, Glitzenstein JS, Jones C, Kolasa J, Likens GE, McDonnell M, Parker GG and Pickett STA (1986) *Long-term Ecological Studies: An Illustrated Account of Their Design, Operation, and Importance to Ecology*. Institute of Ecosystem Studies, Millbrook, New York.

Thompson WL, White GC and Gowan C (1998) *Monitoring Vertebrate Populations*. Academic Press, London.

Vitousek PM and Reiners WA (1975) Ecosystem succession and nutrient retention: a hypothesis. *BioScience* **25**, 376–381.

Walters CJ (1986) *Adaptive Management of Renewable Resources*. Macmillan, New York.

Wiersma GB (ed.) (2004) *Environmental Monitoring*. CRC Press, Boca Raton, Florida.

Yoccoz NG, Nichols JD and Boulinier T (2001) Monitoring of biological diversity in space and time. *Trends in Ecology and Evolution* **16**, 446–453.

Zhan X, Li MY, Zhang Z, Goossens B, Chen Y, Wang H, Bruford M and Wei F (2006) Molecular censusing doubles giant panda population estimate in a key nature reserve. *Current Biology* **16**, R451–452.

Chapter 2

Why monitoring fails

There have been many highly successful long-term ecological monitoring programs. For example, the Lawes Agricultural Trust reported on a series of fertilisation trials in England that have continued since 1843 (Lawes Agricultural Trust 1984). Examples in aquatic ecosystems include Goldman (1981), Schindler *et al.* (1985) and Likens and Bormann (1995) (see Chapters 3 and 4). But along side these effective cases, there is an unfortunate history of poorly planned and unfocused monitoring programs that are either ineffective or fail completely (Orians 1986; Norton 1996; Stankey *et al.* 2003; Nichols and Williams 2006). For example, Allen (1993) and Norton (1996) have described how nearly half of the more than 55 monitoring programs on tussock grasslands in New Zealand were unreported, indicating a failure rate that is extremely high. Similarly, Ward *et al.* (1986) lament about the 'data-rich but information-poor' syndrome in water quality monitoring.

In this chapter, we briefly outline why monitoring programs often fail. These include a lack of questions, poor experimental design, unresolved arguments about what to monitor, over-emphasis on built infrastructure, disengagement of the scientific community, poor data management and breaches of long-term data integrity. We also discuss other factors that contribute to the failure of monitoring programs: lack of funding, the loss of a pivotal person, unexpected problems and excessive bureaucracy. The content of this chapter is a prelude to the following chapter where we propose antidotes to the problems we discuss here.

Table 2.1 Reasons monitoring programs and long-term studies can fail or be ineffective.

Problem	Key reference
Mindless, lacking questions	(Lindenmayer and Likens 2009)
Poor experimental design	(Bernhardt *et al.* 2005)
Monitoring too many things poorly rather than fewer things well	(Zeide 1994)
Failure to agree on what entities to monitor	(Lindenmayer and Likens 2009)
Flawed assumption that all monitoring programs can be the same	This book
Scientific disengagement from monitoring programs	(Franklin *et al.* 1998)
Poor data management	(Caughlan and Oakley 2001)
Loss of integrity of the long-term data record	(Strayer *et al.* 1986)
Lack of funding	(Caughlan and Oakley 2001)
Loss of key personnel	(Kendeigh 1982)
Unexpected major event	(Laurance and Luizao 2007)

CHARACTERISTICS OF INEFFECTIVE MONITORING PROGRAMS

Passive, mindless and lacking questions

Some monitoring programs have been driven by short-term funding or a political directive rather than being underpinned by carefully posed questions and objectives. Nichols and Williams (2006) and Roberts (1991) argued that too often monitoring has been '*planned backwards on the collect now (data), think-later (of a useful question) principle*'. A paucity of questions is a serious problem because it often results in monitoring programs being poorly focused and incapable of delivering effective outcomes (Legg and Nagy 2006; Field *et al.* 2007; Martin *et al.* 2007). In other cases this means that it is not possible to diagnose the cause of a change which, in turn, limits predictive capability either through time or spatially to other landscapes or environments.

An example of the problems created by passive monitoring is that of the Norfolk Island boobook owl (*Ninox novaeseelandiae undulata*). Norfolk Island is a small oceanic island over 350 kilometres east of the city of Brisbane in eastern Australia. It supported a rare island-endemic sub-species of owl. Populations of the species declined over a prolonged period, as revealed by a passive and highly haphazard monitoring program. That

Figure 2.1 Nestlings of hybrids of the Norfolk Island boobook owl and the New Zealand morepork owl. (Photo by Penny Olsen)

work was not guided by any meaningful or tractable scientific questions, nor were there any contrasts in management treatments or interventions to determine the causes of decline, although many possible causes for it were proposed (Olsen 1996). Hence, all that could be surmised from the passive monitoring work was that the population was declining. The result was that the species became functionally extinct when a single individual (a female) remained (Olsen 1996; Norman *et al.* 1998). In 1987, two male New Zealand morepork owls (*Ninox novaeseelandiae novaeseelandiae*) were released on Norfolk Island and one bred with the single remaining Norfolk Island boobook owl and their offspring have assisted a recovery of the population to an estimated ~40 birds (P Olsen, pers.comm.).

Poor experimental design

A second problem has been that monitoring programs have often been very poorly designed at the beginning of a study (Krebs 1991). Good design is an inherently statistical process. But professional statisticians are often left out of the experimental design phases of monitoring programs. Issues are then overlooked such as: (1) calculations of statistical power to detect trends (Reed and Blaustein 1995; Strayer 1999; Foster 2001; Field *et al.* 2007) such as levels of replication of different treatments; (2) minimisation of local prediction error; (3) detectability of particular individual biotic species or chemical element (Yoccoz *et al.* 2001; Pellet and Schmidt 2005; Martin *et al.* 2007); (4) optimisation of field methods and statistical design

(Mac Nally 1997; Joseph *et al.* 2006); **(5)** the importance of contrasts between treatments (e.g. where there is a human intervention and where there is not) (Krebs 1991; Walters 1992; Lindenmayer and Franklin 2002), and **(6)** the value of innovative rotating of sampling methods for increasing inference (Welsh *et al.* 2000).

Poor design has numerous knock-on effects that can result in the failure of a monitoring program (Legg and Nagy 2006). For example, it can lead to the results of work not being written up, or when it is, making it difficult for findings to be published in reputable outlets. Poor design also means that it is difficult to assess the effectiveness of a management intervention (e.g. application of a prescribed burning regime in forest) (Whelan 1995) or a major environmental initiative (e.g. national or even continental agro-environmental schemes) (Kleijn *et al.* 2006; Halkowicz 2008). For example, it is presently not possible to assess the effectiveness of ~$US15 billion worth of projects on river restoration in the USA because of poor experimental design and a lack of rigorous monitoring of interventions designed to improve river and stream environments (Bernhardt *et al.* 2005). Indeed, in ~90% of projects there was no form of assessment or monitoring of project effectiveness and limited data to determine which activities had been successful and which had not (Bernhardt *et al.* 2005). Hence key opportunities for management learning have been lost. In other cases, poorly designed monitoring programs could lead to an incorrect decision being made, such as the down-listing of an endangered species when it should not be (Martin *et al.* 2007).

Snowed by a blizzard of ecological details

A third issue is that the design of monitoring programs is often prefaced by protracted (and frequently unresolved) arguments about what to monitor. One response has been to monitor a large number of things (the so-called 'laundry list'). As outlined in the case studies in Chapter 4, some monitoring programs are indeed based on very extensive lists (Zeide 1994). However, the 'laundry-list' approach can have a range of problems. First, it can divert those responsible for establishing a monitoring program from posing well-crafted and tractable questions. Second, resource and time constraints frequently mean that a poorly focused 'laundry list' will result in many things being monitored badly. It is simply not possible to properly monitor a vast number of entities (Zeide 1994). Third, a 'laundry list' may make a monitoring program too expensive to be sustained financially beyond the short-term and may ultimately lead to its collapse. In cases where the objective of a monitoring program is to assess the impacts of resource management practices (e.g. prescriptions for logging operations), demands to measure a long list of attributes may mean that the costs of a monitoring program are mismatched with the level of economic return from that management practice (Franklin *et al.* 1999). This conflict also can quickly undermine a monitoring program. Finally, a 'laundry-list' approach can create problems with the statistical design of a monitoring program. Monitoring a long list of entities can only ever realistically be done on a few sites, but often a robust statistical design for a monitoring program will sometimes call for many sites to be subject to repeated survey (Walters 1992), such as to provide sufficient statistical power to detect an effect or identify a trend.

We believe that 'laundry lists' should be regarded only as starting points in planning, as they do not reflect the realities of operating or financing a credible monitoring program.

Squabbles about what to monitor – 'It's not monitoring without the mayflies'

An alternative response by some workers to the 'laundry-list' approach has been to argue that 'indicator species' or 'indicator groups' should be the targets of monitoring programs (Sparrow *et al.* 1994; Spellerberg 1994; McLaren *et al.* 1998; Woodward *et al.* 1999; Andersen and Majer 2004; Cantarello and Newton 2008; Dung and Webb 2008). Many would argue that the group of organisms they study is special and any valid monitoring program cannot proceed without including them.

We have found that over 55 major taxonomic groups have been proposed as indicators, ranging from viruses and fungi and bryophytes to invertebrates and virtually all major vertebrate groups (Table 2.2) (Lindenmayer 2009). We found that only very rarely was it explicitly stated: (1) what these species or groups were actually indicative of, particularly at the ecosystem level, and (2) the circumstances where these species or groups were or were not appropriate indicators.

There is a vast literature on indicators and indicator species concepts (including the journal *Ecological Indicators,* which focuses extensively on the topic) and it is far beyond the scope of this book to review them here. We briefly outline five major, problematic issues below.

First, almost all applications of the indicator species concept are highly idiosyncratic; that is, they are organism-specific, landscape-specific or ecosystem-specific. Hence transferability to other groups, landscapes, ecosystems, environmental circumstances or over time is problematic. When circumstances change, the difficult and often time-consuming process of

Table 2.2 Examples of groups suggested to be environmental indicators or biodiversity surrogates. Humans are one group that are noticeably absent from the list! (Adapted from Lindenmayer 2009)

Suggested environmental indicators or biodiversity surrogates	Source
Birds	(Scharenberg 1991; Leach and Recher 1993; Greenwood et al. 1995; Barrett and Davidson 2000; Brooker 2002; Suter et al. 2002; Wakelin and Hill 2007; Braunisch and Suchant 2008; Patthey et al. 2008; Zochler et al. 2008)
Owls	(Milledge et al. 1991)
Waterbirds	(Dickson 1993; Weller 1995; Bowker and Downs 2008)
Parrots	(Leech et al. 2008)
Arboreal marsupials	(Cork et al. 1988; Kavanagh 1991; Milledge et al. 1991)
Marsupials	(Sebastiao and Grelle 2009)
Squirrels	(Koprowski and Nandini 2008)
Large terrestrial mammalian carnivores	(Carroll et al. 2001; Handeland et al. 2008)
Small terrestrial mammals	(Pearce and Venier 2005; Klenner and Sullivan 2009; Phelps and Mcbee 2009)
Deer	(Hanley 1993)
Bats	(Richards 1991; MacSwiney et al. 2008)
Whales	(Hooker et al. 1999)
Reptiles	(Thompson et al. 2008)
Snakes	(Lind and Welsh 2005)
Amphibians	(Blaustein 1994; Welsh and Ollivier 1998; Blaustein and Johnson 2003)
Marine fish	(Codi and Humphrey 2004; Goetz et al. 2008; Letica and Gerardo 2008)
Freshwater fish	(Harris 1995; Department of the Environment and Heritage 2002; Dutterer and Allen 2008; Lasne et al. 2008)
Chaetognatha (Arrowworms)	(Tse et al. 2008)
Arthropods	(Kremen 1992; Kremen et al. 1993; Madden and Fox 1997)
Ants	(Andersen 1993; Oliver et al. 2000; Andersen et al. 2003; Hoffman and Andersen 2003; Andersen and Majer 2004; Underwood and Fischer 2006)
Beetles	(Niemela et al. 1993; Rodriguez et al. 1998; Bouyer and Sana 2007; Sakchoowong et al. 2008; da Silva et al. 2009)
Bees (as pollinators)	(Kevan 1999)
Butterflies	(Kerr et al. 2000; Mac Nally and Fleishman 2002; Maes and van Dyck 2005; Pearman and Weber 2007; Hilbeck et al. 2008)
Corals	(Burt et al. 2008; Wang et al. 2008)

Suggested environmental indicators or biodiversity surrogates	Source
Moths	(Summerville et al. 2004)
Aquatic oligochaetes	(Lin and Yo 2008)
Polychaetes	(Paavo et al. 2008)
Chirononids	(Carew and Pettigrove 2003)
Caddisflies	(de Moor and Ivanov 2008)
Terrestrial amphipods	(Kotze and Lawes 2008)
Freshwater amphipods	(Plenet 1995)
Copepods	(Darnis et al. 2008; Hwang et al. 2009)
Dragonflies	(Sato and Riddiford 2008)
Midges	(Dupuis et al. 2008)
Fruit flies	(Parsons 1991)
Mites	(Caruso et al. 2007; Mori 2008)
Spiders	(Jung et al. 2008a; Jung et al. 2008b)
Aquatic crustaceans	(Lake 1986)
Marine crustaceans	(Chou et al. 2002)
Molluscs	(Scanes 1996; Gladstone 2002; Barnes et al. 2007; Strayer 2008)
Gastropods	(Paavo et al. 2008)
Vascular plants	(Klinka et al. 1989; Sydes 1994; Kremen et al. 1998; Pharo et al. 1999; Lunt 2003; Lunt et al. 2005; Pereira and Cooper 2006; Palo et al. 2008; D'Amato et al. 2009)
Ferns	(Hosseini et al. 2007)
Bryophytes	(Edwards 1986; Kreyling et al. 2008)
Marine algae	(Baldi and Hohenegger 2008)
Macroalgae	(Torres et al. 2008)
Fungi	(Bredesn et al. 1997; Berglund and Edman 2005; Halme et al. 2009)
Ectomycorrhizal fungi	(Walker et al. 2008)
Microphytic crusts	(Eldridge and Rosentreter 1999)
Lichens	(Wolseley and Aguirre-Hudson 1991; Loppi et al. 1998; Rogers and Tryel 2008; Ellis et al. 2009)
Viruses	(Chen et al. 2008)
Bacteria	(Hunt et al. 2008)
Cyanobacteria	(Dixon et al. 2006)
Amoebae	(Booth 2001)
Foraminifera	(Lutz et al. 2008)
Diatoms	(Dixit et al. 1992; Patrick and Palavage 1994; Reid et al. 1995; Ponader and Charles 2007; Dohet et al. 2008)

Figure 2.2 The Yellow-bellied glider. This spectacular wide-ranging gliding arboreal marsupial from Australian forests was proposed as an indicator species of forest suitability for arboreal marsupials and other vertebrates (Milledge *et al.* 1991), but subsequent analyses showed that an average of only two (of a possible seven) other species in the arboreal marsupial assemblage co-occurred with it (Lindenmayer and Cunningham 1997) and the responses of arboreal marsupials to landscape conditions and disturbance regimes proved to be markedly different from those of other groups such as small mammals (Cunningham *et al.* 2005) and birds (Lindenmayer *et al.* 2009). (Photo by David Lindenmayer)

identifying new indicator species must be instigated. For example, there are many cases where a given group is recommended as an indicator species in one environment, but is then found to perform poorly in that surrogate role in another environment or landscape (Sergio *et al.* 2008). Illustrative cases include raptors – Thiollay (1996) and Sergio *et al.* (2008) versus Rodriguez-Estrella (1998) and Roth and Weber (2008); small mammals – Pearce and Venier (2005) versus Lehmkuhl (2008); arboreal marsupials – Milledge *et al.* (1991) versus Lindenmayer and Cunningham (1997) (Figure 2.2); and plants – Gegout and Krizova (2003). Even the same species may respond in markedly different ways in different landscapes (Dooley and Bowers 1998), aquatic ecosystems (Potapova and Charles 2007) or seascapes (Kirby *et al.* 2006).

Second, different species respond in often quite markedly different ways to environmental change. This difference can be true even for closely related species such as those from the same genus or guild. Even the same species may respond in different landscapes, aquatic ecosystems or sea-scapes in markedly different ways (Misra *et al.* 1989; Kirby *et al.* 2006; Potapova and Charles 2007; Lindenmayer *et al.* 2008). Some species are insensitive to change (e.g. Kavanagh and Stanton 2005).

Third, there is a general lack of understanding of causal relationships between indicator species and the entities they are assumed to indicate (Lindenmayer *et al.* 2000; Wright-Stow and Winterbourn 2003). Indeed, in several cases where causal relationships have been carefully examined, a purported indicator species subsequently has proven to be a misleading sur-rogate of environmental conditions or the occurrence of other elements of biota. For example, early research on the bivalve mollusc *Velesunio ambiguus* in Australian rivers suggested that the species was an indicator of heavy metal pollution (Walker 1981). Subsequent work found that the uptake of heavy metals by *V. ambiguus* did not reflect the extent of pollution in the surrounding river system, making the mollusc an unreliable and unsuitable indicator species (Millington and Walker 1983; Maher and Norris 1990).

A fourth problem with the indicator species approach is that there is often poor or vague specification of the environmental conditions for which particular indicators are purported to be indicative of, for example, 'ecosystem health' (Bouyer and Sana 2007), 'disturbed health' (Mario-gomez *et al.* 2006), 'ecosystem vital signs' and 'environmental change' (Dixit *et al.* 1992).

Finally, in many cases there is over-simplified, somewhat misleading and often confusing usage of the term 'indicator' as simply the entity which is being measured (e.g. Woodward *et al.* 1999; State of the Environment Report 2001; The Heinz Center 2008).

An increasing number of studies is highlighting the array of problems associated with biodiversity surrogate approaches such as indicator species, and related concepts such as 'umbrella species' and 'focal species' (Temple and Wiens 1989; Wu and Lau 1996; Lindenmayer *et al.* 2000; Rolstad *et al.* 2002). It is sobering to consider the results of studies by Andelman and Fagan (2000) and Oster *et al.* (2008) that examined the efficacy of the indi-cator species concept and found that its application did not capture more species or better protected habitats than organisms selected at random from the large databases they assembled to conduct their tests! Similarly, Caro *et al.* (2004) found that small reserves in Belize selected on the basis of conserving flagship species were not effective at conserving other ele-ments of the biota, and were no better than reserves selected using non-flagship taxa.

Scepticism of the indicator species and other surrogate approaches is important because it is critical for resource managers, policy-makers and scientists to be made aware that a particular species may not be a good indicator of the presence or abundance of other species, of the suitability of the ecosystem to support species assemblages, or of ecosystem processes. Otherwise they may believe that by conserving a so-called 'indicator species' they have effectively conserved all other biota when in fact they have been deceived by a false sense of management security (Lindenmayer *et al.* 2009).

There is no doubt that particular species and sets of species should be the focus of long-term research and monitoring programs. It would be nonsensical to argue otherwise. But it should not necessarily be assumed that these species or groups of species are necessarily 'indicators' (Underwood and Fischer 2006). Rather, we believe it is better to quantify the direct measure, not assume that measure is a surrogate for something else (Landres *et al.* 1988; Lindenmayer *et al.* 2002), and ensure that the selection of the most appropriate entities to monitor emerges from the questions being asked. We also readily acknowledge, however, that in some circumstances the real-time direct measurement of some entities is not possible. As an example, it is obviously not possible to directly measure paleoclimates or environmental conditions and that species composition of organisms, like diatoms, has been used to reconstruct past climates, ocean conditions and other environmental conditions, such as acid rain (Charles *et al.* 1990).

Assumption that 'one-size-fits-all'

Many scientific articles make recommendations about generic frameworks for monitoring programs. Recommendations are made about lists of entities to be measured and the way they should be measured. These kinds of recommendations are understandable given a desire to create compatibility of data recording and increased coordination and comparison across studies. However, this approach is problematic for a range of reasons.

We believe it is often not appropriate to measure the same entities (e.g. the same species groups or ecosystem function) in different places, which is frequently mandated in 'big science' efforts such as the International Biological Program (IBP). Measuring diverse assemblages of butterflies may well be valid in tropical rainforests where this group can be species rich, but is likely to be of little merit in desert environments where this group may have relatively few representatives. Similarly, the kinds of threatening processes in a tropical savanna and an alpine meadow may be so different that environmental monitoring or biodiversity monitoring programs in them would most likely be very different. Even within the same broad vegetation type (e.g. tropical rainforest), the application of identical monitoring protocols may not be particularly informative because of differences in biota, key ecological processes, or other factors (see also Martins *et al.* 2007).

As we have outlined above, the choice of what entities to measure and how they should be measured is best guided not by a generic framework but rather by well-defined and scientifically tractable questions (see also Martins *et al.* 2007).

Big machines that go 'bing'

> 'An exciting mix of nano-engineered materials, miniaturised computers and rapid wireless communications is giving rise to a new generation of environmental sensors. These new sensors will be able to process information they collect and adapt to changing conditions. They'll be able to measure an amazingly wide range of environmental variables, and they will be able to share this information with a network of sensors. This may be the way of the future for all forms of environmental management, be it catchment management, bushfire risk management, agriculture or monitoring invading pests.'

The above quote is a part of a media release from the Australian Academy of Sciences in late 2008. It suggests that new equipment is the smart science, not the questions being asked to solve a problem. We believe that appropriate equipment is indeed very important for long-term research and monitoring programs, but an over-emphasis on it can be problematic.

A common issue in long-term research and monitoring programs is the focus on building expensive infrastructure (e.g. fences, towers). This infrastructure may create a range of problems and cause monitoring programs to fail. The first is experimental design. When a piece of equipment is expensive there will rarely be many of them, and sometimes only one per catchment, region, state or even nationally. This scarcity, in turn, creates problems for statistical design because it precludes replication, prevents quantification of variability, and limits the spatial extent of inferences that can be made from findings. Second, some kinds of expensive scientific instruments can generate vast quantities of data very quickly. This potential 'overload' can lead to the temptation to do science backwards. That is, data are mined for answers, rather than questions being posed and then data gathered to answer them. In addition, although advancements are rapid, it also can be difficult to know how to analyse veritable mountains of data that are generated from sophisticated pieces of field equipment and then, in turn, use it in applied environmental management (Berkelmans *et al.* 2002). Third, a focus on expensive equipment often fails to recognise that people are the most important infrastructure for maintaining long-term research and monitoring programs. Fourth, the purchase of expensive new equipment may change the way particular entities (e.g. water flows, nutrient levels and animal populations) are measured. This approach can breach the integrity of past data collection and invalidate the continuity of some measures such as time series information (Shapiro and Swain 1983). Fifth, sophisticated equipment can be expensive to maintain. Funding or interest can wane or the equipment can become outdated or superseded and the operators walk away after a relatively short time. This problem may result in little more than littering of the landscape in the long term. Finally, directing large amounts of funding around the need to maintain and operate built infrastructure often occurs at the expense of some other source of scientific funding. Therefore, the opportunity costs of large infrastructure grants may be the reduction of funding for question-based and curiosity-driven science.

Large, sophisticated equipment are powerful data-gathering tools and can make important contributions to long-term research and monitoring. However, as we discuss further in the case studies in Chapter 4, major problems can arise in programs with an excessive focus on built infrastructure. We believe that expenditure on infrastructure should not unjustifiably dominate budgets for long-term research and monitoring programs.

In no way are we opposed to the application of new methods in research and monitoring or the use of sophisticated, expensive field equipment. But the purchase and deployment of such equipment should be justified by the questions asked, and should not jeopardise the funding needed for critical field personnel at the site.

Disengagement

Although scientists have stressed the importance of monitoring for many years in innumerable scientific articles and books, they have often refused to involve themselves directly in monitoring, which they have viewed as the routine collection of data for non-scientific purposes (see Franklin *et al.* 1999). In other cases, scientists have maintained a 'superiority' complex and considered monitoring to be too 'trivial' to warrant their involvement. This prejudice of the scientific community is based on a variety of factors (see Goldsmith 1991; Hellawell 1991), particularly the failure of academic reward systems to recognise and credit involvement in monitoring programs (Taylor *et al.* 1998). The fact that many resource managers do not consider science or scientists to be essential participants in development and operation of their monitoring programs is another problem.

In other cases, scientists do not treat policy-makers with appropriate respect and treat them as 'cash cows' for providing funding to support their 'pet' research projects. However, while scientists may design elegant experiments and other kinds of studies, which go on to produce fascinating papers in high-quality scientific journals, their work may spectacularly fail the 'test of management relevance'. Russell-Smith *et al.* (2003) provide a sobering example of this disconnect in a fire experiment in the savannas of northern Australia, which was published in the prestigious journal *Ecological Monographs*. Although their studies encompassed elegantly designed and replicated experimental plots, key questions about the effects of multiple fires at several spatial scales could not be addressed, even though answers to them were of primary interest and relevance to resource managers (Russell-Smith *et al.* 2003) (J Russell-Smith, pers.comm.). A key part of the problem was that the experiment was designed and implemented without the engagement of landowners and resource managers (Russell-Smith *et al.* 2003). Conversely, resource managers and policy-makers will often have demands to monitor the effectiveness and outcomes of important management interventions and environmental programs, but lack the scientific and statistical skills to do it. Partial failure to demonstrate effectiveness in multi-billion dollar agri-environmental schemes in Europe and Australia has been attributed, in part, to a paucity of scientific engagement with resource managers and the subsequent development of robust and credible monitoring programs (Kleijn and Sutherland 2003; Kleijn *et al.* 2006; Field *et al.* 2007).

In summary, disengagement is a truly substantial issue, particularly from the scientific community. It is also clear that scientists cannot expect engagement from policy-makers and extract significant funds to support monitoring unless they can make a compelling case for it. This case can only be advocated when scientists are able to convince policy-makers that they can overcome problems with experimental design, reach an agreement on what to monitor and provide value to the policy-makers.

Poor data management

Many monitoring programs have failed to employ adequate data management procedures, such as appropriate standards for data documentation, and few have provided adequate financial support (Caughlan and Oakley 2001). A general 'rule of thumb' for data management costs in the US

Long-Term Ecological Research (LTER) program is about 15% of project costs, but some sites are higher and some lower. Some non-LTER recommendations for information management, including data management, in long-term research and monitoring programs are about 20% of total project costs (National Research Council 1995; Stohlgren *et al.* 1995; Jensen and Bourgeron 2001; Lindenmayer and Franklin 2002).

Adequate management of long-term environmental data sets is very challenging and requires substantial technical expertise and significant financial support (Michener and Brunt 2000). Managers and scientists have often failed to recognise the technical challenges, costs, and critical role of data management, preferring to utilise financial resources for other priorities. The reality is that the curation of data is often an after-thought in the vast majority of ecological projects (Caughlan and Oakley 2001). As a consequence, immense amounts of important environmental data, including long-term records, have disappeared or effectively been lost due to inadequate documentation and quality control (Norton 1996). Indeed, one of us (DBL) has personally witnessed several cases where government agencies have discarded high-quality datasets that were subsequently recognised to be extremely important.

Breaches of data integrity

Monitoring programs can fail when the integrity of the data is breached by changes in measurement protocols. There are numerous such cases including the following famous example, which has been published in prestigious journals, cited widely, used in textbooks, and used in litigation (Harris 1986). Schelske and Stoermer (1971) collected together extensive data from 1926 to 1962 showing evidence of significant temporal declines in the amount of dissolved silica in Lake Michigan, which they linked to increased populations of diatoms that they suggested were responding to increased loadings of total phosphorus (eutrophication) in the lake. Dissolved silica is an important nutrient for diatoms. However, Shapiro and Swain (1983) argued that instead, the decline in dissolved silica was due to a change in the analytical method for silica determination and in a change in the laboratories doing the analyses (Figure 2.3). As such, they considered the quality assurance/quality control to be inadequate and therefore they argued that these long-term data were almost worthless. Schelske (1988) countered with a more detailed analysis of the analytical methods and concluded that there had indeed been a significant decrease in dissolved silica during 1954–1969 because of the uptake and sedimentation of silica by diatoms, this process being tightly coupled to phosphorus in

---

BOX 2.1 THE CHALLENGES OF LONG-TERM DATA MANAGEMENT

Some of the challenges of data management from long-term studies are illustrated by the experience in the 26-year forest ecosystem studies in the wet forests of Victoria, Australia (Lindenmayer 2009). Over the duration of the project, the 'evolution' of data storage methods has included magnetic tapes, 5½″ floppy disks, 3 ½″ floppy disks, CDs, DVDs and memory sticks. The time to redundancy of these various storage methods has continued to shorten. The development of new data storage methods has required regular updating, and sometimes complete re-coding of datasets, a process that can lead to errors being introduced to datasets or data loss. Moreover, it is very time-consuming. For example, the re-coding of old data has required very careful checking as error rates otherwise average 7–10% of the total imported information. A revelation in the project has been the importance of primary data, in the form of pencil entries on paper copies of field datasheets. Many errors in digital datasets were rectified only by cross-reference with original field datasheets. The orderly storage of vast quantities of paper records is important, as is its duplication and storage off-site in case of an unforeseen event such as an office fire, a fate not unknown in government agencies and universities.

These same problems and challenges have occurred in the long-term Hubbard Brook Ecosystem Study and we suspect that they are common in most long-term research and monitoring programs.

---

the lake. Schelske *et al.* (1983) further argued that the sediment record in Lake Michigan supported the presence of increased diatoms in the lake. This controversy raged at scientific conferences, in prominent scientific journals and even in the courts for almost two decades before ending at the US Supreme Court (Mortimer 1981). The correct interpretation of these long-term data had high relevance for the management of eutrophication in this highly visible and anthropogenically important Laurentian Great Lake.

Reviewers of the large-scale study of landscape change at Tumut in south-eastern Australia suggested the replacement of volunteer observer surveys of birds by automatic bird call recorders. However, comparison of the two methods revealed that markedly different kinds of data were gathered using the two methods (Cunningham *et al.* 2004). Thus, replacement of one method (human counts) by another (automatic bird call recorders) would have breached the integrity of the long-term data record, making it impossible to conduct a valid interpretation of the temporal changes in bird populations in the study region.

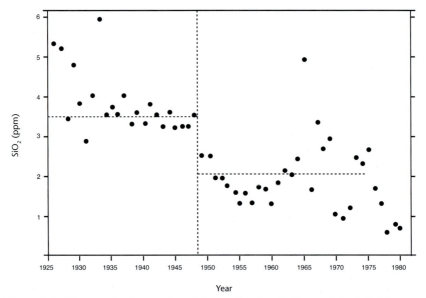

Figure 2.3 Changes in time series data on dissolved silica in Lake Michigan following changes in analytical methods. Vertical line indicates when analytical laboratory was changed. (Modified from Shapiro and Swain 1983)

There are numerous other cases where new methods can dramatically improve field protocols (e.g. DNA-profiling for detecting individual animals) and enhance measures like counts of animal abundance. Indeed, this was the case for the giant panda where molecular methods doubled the known population of the species (Zhan *et al.* 2006). However, this result also meant that it was not possible to compare new counts with past ones and ascertain what changes in abundance (if any) had taken place in response to reservation and management strategies (Zhan *et al.* 2006).

OTHER FACTORS CONTRIBUTING TO INEFFECTIVE MONITORING PROGRAMS

Some monitoring programs may be ineffective for reasons other than the ones summarised above. We touch on four of these in the remainder of this chapter, but are mindful that there are still others which we have not discussed here.

Lack of funding – grant myopia

Short-term funding cycles often emphasise new work rather than long-term studies and at the same time fail to comprehend the profound influence of long-term factors such as site histories and baselines for understanding ecological phenomena (see Gustavsson 2007; Likens and Buso 2009). Therefore, adequate and sustained funding for monitoring programs is rarely available and valuable insights are lost (Caughlan and Oakley 2001). Since monitoring is often directed toward assessing rather than conducting management activities, funds for monitoring typically have low priority. In many cases scientists and policy-makers have failed to calculate the costs of a long-term monitoring program relative to the benefits that it will generate.

Even if adequate funds were provided to plan and initiate a monitoring program (a relatively rare occurrence), most programs have subsequently been starved for financial and logistical resources. As a result, severely under-funded monitoring programs cannot be conducted properly and ultimately fail.

It is very difficult to assure that adequate financial resources will be continuously available. Most government agencies and corporations have annual budget cycles that make monitoring programs, which are necessarily long-term, vulnerable to budget cuts as short-term shifts occur in organisational priorities and objectives. In our experience, monitoring programs are among the first to lose funding during economic downturns. Many organisations are naïve to the long-term financial and logistical implications of establishing a monitoring program (Walsh and White 1999) and unaware that:

'Monitoring sustainability will only be possible if the monitoring system is itself sustainable'

Watson and Novelly 2004: 16

A shortage of funding for long-term monitoring is particularly severe in some kinds of marine monitoring such as in deep sea environments where the costs are extremely high.

The loss of a champion

Many monitoring programs fail when the leader or champion for the work leaves, retires or dies (Strayer *et al.* 1986; Norton 1996). For example, the 27-year-long studies of birds in the forests of central Illinois by Kendeigh (1982) stopped in 1976 when he retired (Strayer *et al.* 1986). Garcia and Lescuyer (2008) describe how the handing over of large institutional monitoring programs to local communities of people nearly always results in these programs failing quickly. This problem results because of the departure of the champion for a project and loss of the ongoing impetus of the work as well as a failure to engage with local stakeholders. These kinds of failures reflect the failure of organisations to institutionalise monitoring programs (Lindenmayer and Franklin 2002).

Out of nowhere

An unforeseen natural disaster or a major human disturbance can threaten long-term research and monitoring programs. For example, Laurance and Luizao (2007) describe how the Manaus-Venezuela Highway is threatening the integrity of the 30-year Biological Diversity of Forest Fragments Project (BDFFP) near Manaus, Brazil (Figure 2.4). Many important new insights have been derived from this major study of how different groups of biota respond to landscape modification and habitat fragmentation (Laurance *et al.* 1997). Analogous results were observed following major hurricane devastation in Puerto Rico (Basnet *et al.* 1992). Likens (1985) describes a similar experience to that in Brazilian Amazonia in which the development of an interstate highway through the White Mountains of New Hampshire, USA led to major changes in the integrity of Mirror Lake and its catchment that had been studied for seven years previously (Likens 1985; Rosenberry *et al.* 2007; Likens and Buso 2009).

There are other cases where a major disturbance can trigger exciting opportunities for ecological studies that lead to important new scientific discoveries and insights. The 1980 volcanic eruption at Mt St Helens and the wildfires at Yellowstone National Park in 1988 in the USA are classic examples. Post-disturbance work in these places resulted in new perspectives on disturbance theory, ecological succession and ecosystem recovery (Franklin and MacMahon 2000; Turner *et al.* 2003; Dale *et al.* 2005).

Excessive bureaucracy

As successful long-term monitoring programs age, they can get bigger and involve more projects and more people. More of the science is then run by committees and more meetings are required to maintain communication across a large group of researchers and administrators. More projects mean more and larger datasets and therefore data management and data sharing. Intellectual property issues assume greater importance. Increased competition, rather than cooperation (especially among state and federal agencies), can become very counterproductive for the results of long-term monitoring. More people and more projects mean that more grants are required to generate the funds to continue the work. Each of these factors indicates that the bureaucracy involved in maintaining long-term monitoring programs can increase over time. When this bureaucracy is not carefully managed,

Figure 2.4 The Manaus-Venezuela Highway – a major road development which is threatening the integrity of the Biological Diversity of Forest Fragments Project (BDFFP) near Manaus, Brazil. (Photo courtesy of Bill Laurance)

monitoring programs that have been successful can ultimately fail because of an increasing focus on 'busy work' rather than science.

Another less obvious, but no less real impediment to long-term monitoring is what might be called the loss of the cultural infrastructure. A field site that might appear to administrators or bureaucrats to have 'spartan' or even unsafe living quarters and/or laboratory facilities, in fact may be the 'heart' of innovative and productive science for the project, allowing scientists to work and live together while doing research, adjacent to the research site. This certainly was the case in the early days of the Hubbard Brook Ecosystem Study where scientists lived, worked and thought together in the old Pleasant View Farmhouse at the base of the Hubbard Brook Valley. It was true in the famous, long-term studies at the Experimental Lakes Area in Ontario as well, where scientists 'worked full-time, brainstorming late into the night' at a remote facility in Canada (Stokstad 2008). The so-called, 'Darwin Cabin', which had been used so effectively to develop and brainstorm ideas by the Trophic Cascade Project at a remote University of Notre Dame Environmental Research Center in northern Michigan, USA, has just been torn down to 'upgrade facilities'. It remains to be seen what impact this change will have on the very productive science stemming from this outstanding project.

SUMMARY

Any one or a combination of factors may make monitoring fail. Ineffective monitoring programs can be characterised by one or more of the following 'features':

- failure to set achievable objectives
- lack of tractable scientific questions
- deficiencies in experimental design
- lack of agreement on which ecological entities to monitor
- disengagement of key parties – policy-makers, resource managers and scientists
- inattention to data management and data quality
- maintaining data integrity over long periods
- excessive bureaucracy and squabbles about intellectual property
- loss of the champion for a project.

These characteristics mean that it can be difficult to determine when it is appropriate for a monitoring program to continue, to cease, or when the program can be modified and made more effective during the study.

Well-designed and implemented monitoring programs that do not have these characteristics may still fail for other reasons such as a lack of funding, and an unforeseen event like a major human or natural disturbance (although the latter can sometimes provide research and monitoring opportunities). As a result of these numerous problems and the frequent lack of agreement among scientists about what to monitor, there is little wonder that decision-makers may be hesitant to fund monitoring programs. With so many opportunities for failure, some readers may wonder whether any monitoring programs have been successful, a topic we turn to in the next chapter.

REFERENCES

Allen RB (1993) An appraisal of monitoring studies in South Island tussock grasslands, New Zealand. *New Zealand Journal of Ecology* **17**, 61–63.

Andelman SJ and Fagan WF (2000) Umbrellas and flagships: efficient conservation surrogates or expensive mistakes? *Proceedings of the National Academy of Sciences of the United States of America* **97**, 5954–5959.

Andersen AA, Hoffman BD and Somes J (2003) Ants as indicators of minesite restoration: community recovery at one of eight rehabilitation sites in central Queensland. *Ecological Management and Restoration* **S4**, S12–19.

Andersen AN (1993) Ants as indicators of restoration success at a uranium mine in tropical Australia. *Restoration Ecology* **12**, 156–167.

Andersen AN and Majer JD (2004) Ants show the way Down Under: invertebrates as bioindicators in land management. *Frontiers in Ecology and the Environment* **2**, 291–298.

Baldi K and Hohenegger J (2008) Paleoecology of benthic foraminifera of the Baden-Sooss section (Bandenian, Middle Mioecene, Vienna Basin, Austria). *Geologica Carpathica* **59**, 411–424.

Barnes TK, Volety AK, Chartier K, Mazzotti FJ and Pearlstine L (2007) A habitat suitability index model for the Eastern Oyster (*Crassostrea virginica*), a tool for restoration of the Caloosahatchee Estuary, Florida. *Journal of Shellfish Research* **26**, 949–959.

Barrett G and Davidson I (2000) Community monitoring of woodland habitats - the Birds on Farms survey. In *Temperate Eucalypt Woodlands in Australia: Biology, Conservation, Management and Restoration.* (Eds RJ Hobbs and CJ Yates) pp. 382–399. Surrey Beatty and Sons, Chipping Norton.

Basnet K, Likens GE, Scatena FN and Lugo AE (1992) Hurricane Hugo: damage to a tropical rain forest in Puerto Rico. *Journal of Tropical Ecology* **8**, 47–56.

Berglund H and Edman M (2005) Temporal variation in wood-fungi diversity in boreal old-growth forests: implications for monitoring. *Ecological Applications* **15**, 970–982.

Berkelmans R, Hendee JC, Marshall PA, Ridd PV, Orpin AR and Irvone D (2002) Automatic weather stations: tools for managing and monitoring potential impacts to coral reefs. *Marine Technology Society Journal* **36**, 29–38.

Bernhardt ES, Palmer MA and Allan JD (2005) Synthesizing US river restoration projects. *Science* **308**, 636–637.

Blaustein AR (1994) Chicken Little or Nero's fiddle? A perspective on declining amphibian populations. *Herpetologica* **50**, 85–97.

Blaustein AR and Johnson PTJ (2003) Explaining frog deformities. *Scientific American* **288**, 60–65.

Booth RK (2001) Ecology of testate amoebae (Protozoa) in two Lake Superior coastal wetlands: implications for paleoecology and environmental monitoring *Wetlands* **21**, 564–576.

Bouyer J and Sana Y (2007) Identification of ecological indicators for monitoring ecosystem health in the Trans-boundary W Regional Park: a pilot study. *Biological Conservation* **138**, 73–88.

Bowker MB and Downs CT (2008) Fluctuations in numbers of Great White Pelicans at Lake St. Lucia in response to changing water levels. *African Journal of Ecology* **46**, 282–90.

Braunisch V and Suchant R (2008) Using ecological forest site mapping for long-term habitat suitability assessments in wildlife conservation – demonstrated for Capercaillie (*Tetrao urogallus*). *Forest Ecology and Management* **256**, 1209–1221.

Bredesn B, Haugan R, Anderaa R, Lindbald I, Okland B and Rosok O (1997) Wood-inhabiting fungi as indicators of ecological continuity within Spruce forests of southeastern Norway. *Blyttia (Oslo)* **54**, 131–140.

Brooker L (2002) The application of focal species knowledge to landscape design in agricultural lands. *Landscape and Urban Planning* **60**, 185–210.

Burt J, Bartholomew A and Usseglio P (2008) Recovery of corals a decade after a bleaching event in Dubai, United Arab Emirates. *Marine Biology* **154**, 27–36.

Cantarello E and Newton AC (2008) Identifying cost-effective indicators to assess the conservation status of forested habitats in Natura 2000 sites. *Forest Ecology and Management* **256**, 815–826.

Carew ME and Pettigrove V (2003) Identifying chirononomids (*Diperta: Chirononimidae*) for biological monitoring with PCR-RLFP. *Bulletin of Entomological Research* **93**, 483–490.

Caro T, Engilis A, Fitzherbert E and Gardner T (2004) Preliminary assessment of the flagship species concept at a small scale. *Animal Conservation* **7**, 63–70.

Carroll C, Noss RF and Paquet PC (2001) Carnivores as focal species for conservation planning in the Rocky Mountain region. *Ecological Applications* **11**, 961–980.

Caruso T, Pigino G, Bernini F, Bargagli R and Migliorini M (2007) The Berger-Parker index as an effective tool for monitoring the biodiversity of disturbed soils: a case study on Mediterranean oribatid (*Acari: Oribatida*) assemblage. *Biodiversity and Conservation* **16** 3277–3285.

Caughlan L and Oakley KL (2001) Cost considerations for long-term ecological monitoring. *Ecological Indicators* **1**, 123–134.

Charles DF, Binford MW, Furlong ET, Hites RA, Mitchell MJ, Norton SA, Oldfield F, Paterson MJ, Smol JP, Uutala AJ, White JR, Whitehead DR and Wise RJ (1990) Paleoecological investigation of recent lake acidification in the Adirondack Mountains, NY. *Journal of Paleolimnology* **3**, 195–241.

Chen CY, Shi Y, Li MY, Adams MJ and Chen J-P (2008) A new potyvirus from butterfly flower (*Iris japonica*) in Zhejiang, China. *Archives of Virology* **153**, 567–69.

Chou CL, Haya K, Paon LA, Burridge L and Moffatt JD (2002) Aquaculture-related trace metals in sediments and lobsters and relevance to environmental monitoring program ratings for near-field effects. *Marine Pollution Bulletin* **44**, 1259–1268.

Codi S and Humphrey C (2004) Barramundi as an indicator species for environmental monitoring in north Queensland, Australia: laboratory versus field studies. *Environmental Toxicology and Chemistry* **23**, 2737–2744.

Cork SJ, Margules CR and Braithwaite LW (1988) Implications of Koala nutrition and the ecology of other arboreal marsupials in south-eastern NSW for the conservation management of Koalas. Paper presented at 'Proceedings of the Koala Summit', University of Sydney, 7–8 November 1988. (Eds D Lunney, C Urquhart and P Read), pp. 48–57.

Cunningham RB, Lindenmayer DB and Lindenmayer BD (2004) Sound recording of bird vocalisations in forests. I. Relationships between bird vocalisations and point interval counts of bird numbers – a case study in statistical modeling. *Wildlife Research* **31**, 195–207.

Cunningham RB, Lindenmayer DB, MacGregor C, Welsh AW and Barry S (2005) Small mammal populations in a wet eucalypt forest. Factors influencing the probability of capture. *Wildlife Research* **32**, 657–671.

D'Amato AW, Orwig DA and Foster DR (2009) Understorey vegetation in old-growth and second-growth *Tsuga canadensis* forests in western Massachusetts *Forest Ecology and Management* **257**, 1043–1052.

da Silva PM, Aguiar CA, Niemela J, Soussa JP and Serrano AR (2009) Cork-oak woodlands as key habitats for biodiversity conservation in Mediterranean landscapes: a case study using rove and ground beetles (*Coleoptera: Staphylinidae, Carabidae*). *Biodiversity and Conservation* **18**, 605–619.

Dale V, Swanson FJ and Crisafulli CM (2005) *Ecological Responses to the 1980 Eruptions of Mt. St. Helens*. Springer-Verlag, New York.

Darnis G, Barber DG and Fortier L (2008) Sea ice and the onshore-offshore gradient in pre-winter zooplantkon assemblages in southeastern Beaufort Sea. *Journal of Marine Systems* **74**, 994–1011.

de Moor FC and Ivanov VD (2008) Global diversity of caddisflies (*Trichoptera: Insecta*) in freshwater. *Hydrobiologica* **595**, 393–407.

Department of the Environment and Heritage (2002) *Annual Report of the Supervising Scientist 2000-2001*. Commonwealth of Australia, Canberra.

Dickson DL (1993) The Red-throated Loon as an indicator of environmental quality. *Canadian Wildlife Service Occasional Paper* **73**, 1–17.

Dixit SS, Smol JP, Kingston JC and Charles DF (1992) Diatoms- powerful indicators of environmental change. *Environmental Science and Technology* **26**, 22–33.

Dixon LK, Vargo GA, Johansson JO, Montgomery R and Neely MB (2006) Trends and explanatory variables for the major phytoplankton groups of two southwestern Florida estuaries. USA *Journal of Sea Research* **61**, 95–102.

Dohet D, Ector L, Cauchie HM and Hoffmann L (2008) Identification of benthic invertebrate and diatom indicator taxa that distinguish different stream types as well as degraded from reference conditions in Luxembourg. *Animal Biology* **58**, 419–472.

Dooley JL and Bowers MA (1998) Demographic responses to habitat fragmentation: experimental tests at the landscape and patch scale. *Ecology* **79**, 969–980.

Dung NT and Webb EL (2008) Combining local ecological knowledge and quantitative forest surveys to select indicator species for forest condition in Central Vietnam. *Ecological Indicators* **8**, 767–770.

Dupuis DD, Svensson JE and Taylor DJ (2008) The cryptic origins of environment-indiacting phantom midges (Chaoborus). *Limnology and Oceanography* **53** 236–243.

Dutterer AC and Allen MS (2008) Spotted sunfish habitat selection at three Florida Rivers and implications for minimum flows. *Transactions of the American Fisheries Society* **137**, 454–466.

Edwards ME (1986) Disturbance history of four Snowdonian woodlands and their relation to Atlantic bryophyte distributions. *Biological Conservation* **37**, 301–320.

Eldridge DJ and Rosentreter R (1999) Morphological groups: a framework for monitoring microphytic crusts in arid landscapes *Journal of Arid Environments* **41**, 11–25.

Ellis CJ, Yahr R and Coppins BJ (2009) Local extent of old-growth woodland modifies ephiphytic response to climate change *Journal of Biogeography* **36**, 302–13.

Field SA, O'Connor PJ, Tyre AJ and Possingham HP (2007) Making monitoring meaningful. *Austral Ecology* **32**, 485–491.

Foster JR (2001) Statistical power in forest monitoring. *Forest Ecology and Management* **151**, 211–222.

Franklin JF, Harmon ME and Swanson FJ (1998) Complementary roles of research and monitoring: lessons from the U.S. LTER Program and Tierra del Fuego. Paper presented at 'North American Science Symposium: Toward a Unified Framework for Inventorying and Monitoring Forest Ecosystem Resources', Guadalajara, Mexico, 1–6 November 1998.

Franklin JF, Harmon ME and Swanson FJ (1999) Complementary roles of research and monitoring: lessons from the U.S. LTER Program and Tierra del Fuego. Paper presented to the Symposium. Paper presented at 'Toward a unified framework for inventorying and monitoring forest ecosystem resources', Guadalajara, Mexico, November 1998.

Franklin JF and MacMahon JA (2000) Messages from a mountain. *Science* **288**, 1183–1185.

Garcia CA and Lescuyer G (2008) Monitoring, indicators and community based forest monitoring in the tropics: pretexts or red herrings? *Biodiversity and Conservation* **17**, 1303–1317.

Gegout J and Krizova E (2003) Comparision of indicator values of forest understorey plant species in Western Carpathians (Slovakia) and Vosges Mountains (France). *Forest Ecology and Management* **182**, 1–11.

Gladstone W (2002) The potential value of indicator groups in the selection of marine reserves. *Biological Conservation* **104**, 211–220.

Goetz A, Cowley PD and Winker H (2008) Selected fishery and population parameters of eight shore-angling species in the Tsitsikamma National Park of no-take marine reserve. *African Journal of Marine Science* **30**, 519–532.

Goldman C (1981) Lake Tahoe: two decades of change in a nitrogen deficient oligo-trophic lake. *Verhandlungen der Internationalen Vereinigung für Theoretische und Angewandte Limnologie* **21**, 45–70.

Goldsmith B (1991) *Monitoring for Conservation and Ecology.* Chapman and Hall, London.

Greenwood J, Baille SR, Gregory RD, Peach WJ and Fuller RJ (1995) Some new approaches to conservation monitoring of British breeding birds. *Ibis* **137**, S16–S28.

Gustavsson E (2007) Land use more than 200 years ago explains current grassland plant diversity in a Swedish agricultural landscape. *Biological Conservation* **138**, 47–59.

Halkowicz S (2008) The evolution of Australia's natural resource management pro-grams: Towards improved targeting and evaluation of investments. *Land Use Policy* **26**, 471–478.

Halme P, Kptiaho JS, lisirno AL, Hottola J, Junninen K, Kouki J, Lindgren M, Monkonnen M, Pentilla R, Renvall P, Siitonen J and Simila M (2009) Perennial polypores as indicators of annual and red-listed polypores. *Ecological Indicators* **9**, 256–66.

Handeland K, Nesse LL, Lillehaug A, Vikoren T, Djonne B and Bergsjo B (2008) Natu-ral and experimental Salmonella typhimurium infections in foxes (*Vulpes vulpes*). *Veterinary Microbiology* **132**, 129–134.

Hanley TA (1993) Balancing economic development, biological conservation, and human culture: the Sitka Black-tailed Deer Odocoileus hemionus sitkensis as an ecological indicator. *Biological Conservation* **66**, 61–67.

Harris GP (1986) *Phytoplankton Ecology, Structure, Function and Fluctuation*. Chapman and Hall, London.

Harris JH (1995) The use of fish in ecological assessments. *Australian Journal of Ecology* **20**, 65–80.

Hellawell JM (1991) Development of a rationale for monitoring. In *Monitoring for Conservation and Ecology*. (Ed FB Goldsmith) pp. 1–14. Chapman and Hall, London.

Hilbeck A, Meier M and Benzler A (2008) Identifying indicator species for post-release monitoring of genetically modified, herbicide resistant crops *Euphytica* **164**, 903–912.

Hoffman BD and Andersen AN (2003) Responses of ants to disturbance in Australia, with particular reference to functional groups. *Austral Ecology* **28**, 444–464.

Hooker SK, Whitehead H and Gowans S (1999) Marine protected area design and the spatial and temporal distribution of cetaceans in a submarine canyon. *Conservation Biology* **13**, 592–602.

Hosseini SM, Moghaddam ER, Akbarinia M and Jalali SA (2007) Phytosociological study of ferns in the central Caspian forests of Iran. *Ekoloji* **16** 74–76.

Hunt WF, Smith JT, Jadlocki SJ, Hathaway JM and Eubanks PR (2008) Pollutant removal and peak flow mitigation by a bioretention cell in urban Charlotte, NC. *Journal of Environmental Engineering* **134**, 403–408.

Hwang J, Souissi S, Dahms H, Tseng L, Schmitt FG and Chen QC (2009) Rank-abundance allocations as a tool to analyze planktonic copepod assemblages off the Dansheui River Estuary (Northern Taiwan). *Zoological Studies* **48**, 49–62.

Jensen ME and Bourgeron PS (Eds) (2001) *A Guidebook for Integrated Ecological Assessments*. Springer-Verlag, New York.

Joseph L, Field SA, Wilcox C and Possingham HP (2006) Presence-absence versus abundance data for monitoring threatened species. *Conservation Biology* **20**, 1679–1687.

Jung MP, Kim ST, Kim H and Lee JH (2008a) The biodiversity and community structure of ground-dwelling spiders in four different field margin types of agricultural landscapes in Korea. *Applied Soil Ecology* **38**, 185–195.

Jung MP, Kim ST, Kim H and Lee JH (2008b) Species diversity and community structure of ground-dwelling spiders in unpolluted and moderately heavy metal-polluted habitats *Water and Soil Pollution*, **195**, 15–22.

Kavanagh RP (1991) The target species approach to wildlife management: gliders and owls in the forests of southeastern New South Wales. In *Conservation of Australia's Forest Fauna*. (Ed. D Lunney) pp. 377–383. Royal Zoological Society of NSW, Sydney.

Kavanagh RP and Stanton, MA (2005) Vertebrate species assemblages and species sensitivity to logging in the forests of north-eastern New South Wales. *Forest Ecology and Management* **209**, 309–341.

Kendeigh SC (1982) Bird populations in east central Illinois: fluctuations, variations and developments over half a century. *Illinois Bird Monographs* **52**, 1–152.

Kerr JT, Sugar A and Packer L (2000) Indicator taxa, rapid biodiversity assessment, and nestedness in an endangered ecosystem. *Conservation Biology* **14**, 1726–1734.

Kevan PG (1999) Pollinators as bioindicators of the state of the environment: species, activity, diversity. *Agriculture Ecosystems and Environment* **74**, 373–393.

Kirby MF, Smith AJ, Barry J, Katsiadaki I, Lyons B and Scott AP (2006) Differential sensitivity of Flounder (*Platichthys flesus*) in response to oestrogenic chemical exposure: An issue for the design and interpretation of monitoring and research programmes. *Marine Environmental Research* **62**, 315–325.

Kleijn D, Baquero RA, Clough Y, Diaz M, De Estaban J, Fernandez F, Gabriel D, Herzog F, Holzchuh A, Johl R, Knop E, Kruess A, Marshall EJ, Steffan-Dewenter I, Tscharntke T, Verhulst J, West TM and Yela JL (2006) Mixed biodiversity benefits of agri-environment schemes in five European countries. *Ecology Letters* **9**, 243–254.

Kleijn D and Sutherland WJ (2003) How effective are European agri-environment schemes in conserving and promoting biodiversity? *Journal of Applied Ecology* **40**, 947–969.

Klenner W and Sullivan TP (2009) Partial and clearcut harvesting of dry Douglas-fir forests: implications for small mammal communities. *Forest Ecology and Management* **257**, 1078–1086.

Klinka K, Krajina VJ, Ceska A and Scagel AM (1989) *Indicator Plants of Coastal British Columbia*. UBC Press, Vancouver.

Koprowski JL and Nandini R (2008) Global hotspots and knowledge gaps for tree and flying squirrels. *Current Science* **95**, 851–856.

Kotze DJ and Lawes MJ (2008) Environmental indicator potential of the dominant litter decomposer, Talitriator africana (Crustacea, Amphipoda) in Afrotemperate forests. *Austral Ecology* **33**, 737–746.

Krebs CJ (1991) The experimental paradigm and long-term population studies. *Ibis* **133**, 2–8.

Kremen C (1992) Assessing the indicator properties of species assemblages for natural areas monitoring. *Ecological Applications* **2**, 203–217.

Kremen C, Colwell RK, Erwin TL, Murphy DD, Noss RF and Sanjayan MA (1993) Terrestrial arthropod assemblages – their use in conservation planning. *Conservation Biology* **7**, 796–808.

Kremen C, Raymond I and Lance K (1998) An interdisciplinary tool for monitoring conservation impacts in Madagascar. *Conservation Biology* **12**, 549–563.

Kreyling J, Schmiedinger A, Macdonald E and Beierkuhnlein C (2008) Slow understory redevelopment after clearcutting in high mountain forests. *Biodiversity and Conservation* **17**, 2339–2355.

Lake PS (1986) *Ecology of the Yabby Cherax destructor Clark Crustacea: Decapoda: Parastacidae and its Potential as a Sentinel Animal for Mercury and Lead Pollution.* Australian Government Publishing Service, Canberra.

Landres PB, Verner J and Thomas JW (1988) Ecological uses of vertebrate indicator species: a critique. *Conservation Biology* 2, 316–328.

Lasne E, Bergerot B, Lek S and Laffaille P (2008) Fish zonation and indicator species for the evaluation of the ecological status of rivers: examples of the Loire Basin (France). *River Research and Applications* 23, 877–890.

Laurance W and Luizao R (2007) Driving a edge into the Amazon. *Nature* 448, 409–410.

Laurance WF, Bierregaard RO, Gascon C, Didham RK, Smith AP, Lynam AJ, Viana VM, Lovejoy TE, Sieving KE, Sites JW, Andersen M, Tocher MD, Kramer EA, Restrepo C and Moritz C (1997) Tropical forest fragmentation: synthesis of a diverse and dynamic discipline. In *Tropical Forest Remnants. Ecology, Management and Conservation of Fragmented Communities.* (Eds WF Laurance and RO Bierregaard) pp. 502–525. University of Chicago Press, Chicago.

Lawes Agricultural Trust (1984) *Rothamsted: The Classical Experiments.* Rothamsted Agricultural Experiment Station, Rothamsted, England.

Leach GJ and Recher HF (1993) Use of roadside remnants of softwood scrub vegetation by birds in south-eastern Queensland. *Wildlife Research* 20, 233–249.

Leech TJ, Gormley AM and Seddon PJ (2008) Estimating the minimum viable population size of Kaka (*Nestor meridionalis*) a potential surrogate species in New Zealand lowland forest. *Biological Conservation* 141, 681–691.

Legg,CJ and Nagy L (2006) Why most conservation monitoring is, but need not be, a waste of time. *Journal of Environmental Management* 78, 194–199.

Lehmkuhl JF, Peffer RD and O'Connell MA (2008) Riparian and upland small mammals on the east slope of the Cascade Range, Washington. *Northwest Science* 82, 94–107.

Letica AG and Gerardo GB (2008) Determination of esterase activity and characterization of cholinesterases in the reef fish *Haemulon plumeri*. *Ecotoxicology and Environmental Safety,* 67, 787–797.

Likens GE (Ed) (1985) *An Ecosystem Approach to Aquatic Ecology: Mirror Lake and its Environment.* Springer-Verlag, New York.

Likens GE and Bormann FH (1995) *Biogeochemistry of a Forested Ecosystem.* Second edition. Springer-Verlag, New York.

Likens GE and Buso DC (2009) Long-term changes in streamwater chemistry following disturbance in the Hubbard Brook Experimental Forest, USA. *Verhandlungen der Internationalen Vereinigung für Theoretische und Angewandte Limnologie* 30, In press.

Lin KJ and Yo SP (2008) The effect of organic pollution on the abundance and distribution of aquatic oligochaetes in an urban water basin, Taiwan. *Hydrobiologica* **596**, 213–223.

Lind AJ and Welsh HH (2005) Garter Snake population dynamics from a 16-year study: considerations for ecological monitoring. *Ecological Applications* **15**, 294–303.

Lindenmayer DB (2009) *Forest Pattern and Ecological Process: A Synthesis of 25 Years of Research*. CSIRO Publishing, Melbourne.

Lindenmayer DB and Cunningham RB (1997) Patterns of co-occurrence among arboreal marsupials in the forests of central Victoria, southeastern Australia. *Australian Journal of Ecology* **22**, 340–346.

Lindenmayer DB, Cunningham RB, Donnelly CF and Lesslie R (2002) On the use of landscape indices as ecological indicators in fragmented forests. *Forest Ecology and Management* **159**, 203–216.

Lindenmayer DB, Cunningham RB, MacGregor C, Crane M, Michael D, Montague-Drake R, Fischer J, Felton A and Manning A (2008) The changing nature of bird populations in woodland remnants as a pine plantation emerges: results from a large-scale 'natural experiment' of landscape context effects. *Ecological Monographs* **78**, 567–590.

Lindenmayer DB and Franklin JF (2002) *Conserving Forest Biodiversity: A Comprehensive Multiscaled Approach*. Island Press, Washington, DC.

Lindenmayer DB and Likens GE (2009) Are indicator species useful or diversionary? *Journal of Applied Ecology*, (In review).

Lindenmayer DB, Margules CR and Botkin DB (2000) Indicators of biodiversity for ecologically sustainable forest management. *Conservation Biology* **14**, 941–950.

Lindenmayer DB, Wood J, Cunningham RB, McBurney L, Crane M, Montague-Drake R, Michael D and MacGregor C (2009) Are gullies best for biodiversity? An empirical examination of Australian wet forest types: a case study from the wet ash forests of Victoria, south-eastern Australia. *Forest Ecology and Management*, (In press).

Loppi S, Putorti E, Signorini C, Fommei S, Pirintsos SA and de Dominicis V (1998) A retrospective study using epiphytic lichens as biomonitors of air quality: 1980 and 1996 (Tuscany, central Italy). *Acta Oecologica* **19**, 405–408.

Lunt I (2003) A protocol for integrated management, monitoring and enhancement of degraded Themeda triandra grassland based on plantings of indicator species. *Restoration Ecology* **11**, 223–230.

Lunt I, Coates F and Spooner P (2005) Grassland indicator species predict flowering of endangered Gaping Leek-orchid (*Prasophyllum correctum* D.L. Jones). *Ecological Restoration and Management* **6**, 69–71.

Lutz BP, Ishman SE, McNeill DF, Klaus J and Budd AF (2008) Late Neogene planktonic foraminifera of the Ciboa Valley (northern Dominican Republic): Biostratigraphy and paleoceanography. *Marine Micropaleontology* **69**, 282–296.

Mac Nally R (1997) Monitoring forest bird communities for impact assessment – the influence of sampling intensity and spatial scale. *Biological Conservation* **82**, 355–367.

Mac Nally R and Fleishman E (2002) Using 'indicator' species to model species richness: model development and predictions. *Ecological Applications* **12**, 79–92.

MacSwiney MC, Clarke FM and Racey PA (2008) What you see is not what you get: the role of ultrasonic detectors in increasing inventory completeness in Neotropical bat assemblages. *Journal of Applied Ecology* **45**, 1364–1371.

Madden KE and Fox BJ (1997) Arthropods as indicators of the effects of flouride pollution on the succession following sand mining. *Journal of Applied Ecology* **34**, 1239–1256.

Maes D and van Dyck H (2005) Habitat quality and biodiversity indicator performances of a threatened butterfly versus a multispecies group for wet heathlands in Belgium. *Biological Conservation* **123**, 177–187.

Maher W and Norris RH (1990) Water quality assessment programs in Australia: deciding what to measure and how and where to use bioindicators. *Environmental Monitoring and Assessment* **14**, 115–130.

Mariogomez I, Soto M, Cancio I, Orbea A, Garmedndia L and Cajaraville MP (2006) Cell and tissue markers in mussel, histopathology in hake and anchovy from Bay of Biscay after Prestige Oil spill (monitoring campaign 2003). *Marine Pollution Bulletin* **53**, 287–304.

Martin J, Kitchens WM and Hines JE (2007) Importance of well-designed monitoring programs for the conservation of endangered species: Case study of the Snail Kite. *Conservation Biology* **21**, 472–481.

Martins S, Sanderson JG and Silva-Junior J (2007) Monitoring mammals in the Caxiuana National Forest, Brazil – first results from the Tropical Ecology, Assessment and Monitoring (TEAM) program. *Biodiversity and Conservation* **16**, 857–870.

McLaren MA, Thompson ID and Baker JA (1998) Selection of vertebrate wildlife indicators for monitoring sustainable forest management in Ontario. *Forestry Chronicle* **74**, 241–248.

Michener WK and Brunt JW (2000) *Ecological Data: Design, Management and Processing.* Blackwell Science, Oxford.

Milledge DR, Palmer CL and Nelson JL (1991) Barometers of change: the distribution of large owls and gliders in Mountain Ash forests of the Victorian Central Highlands and their potential as management indicators. In *Conservation of Australia's Forest Fauna.* (Ed. D Lunney) pp. 53–65. Royal Zoological Society of New South Wales, Sydney.

Millington PJ and Walker KF (1983) Australian freshwater mussel *Velesunio ambiguus* (Phillipi) as a biological indicator for zinc, iron and manganese. *Australian Journal of Marine and Freshwater Research* **34**, 873–892.

Misra RK, Uthe JF and Vynke W (1989) Monitoring of time trends in contaminant levels using a multispecies approach – Contaminant trends in Atlantic Cod (*Gadus morhua*) and European Flounder (*Platichthys flesus*) on the Belgian coast, 1978–1985. *Marine Pollution Bulletin* **20**, 500–502.

Mori SR (2008) Response of forest soil Acari to prescribed fire following stand structure manipulation in the Southern Cascade Range *Canadian Journal of Forest Research* **38**, 956–968.

Mortimer CH (1981) The Lake Michigan Pollution Case. Sea Grant Institute and Center for Great Lakes Studies. University of Wisconsin.

National Research Council (1995) Finding the Forest in the Trees: The Challenge of Combining Diverse Environmental Data. National Research Council, Washington, DC.

Nichols JD and Williams BK (2006) Monitoring for conservation. *Trends in Ecology and Evolution* **21**, 668-673.

Niemela J, Langor D and Spence JR (1993) Effects of clear-cut harvesting on boreal ground-beetle assemblages (Coleoptera: Carabidae) in western Canada. *Conservation Biology* **7**, 551–561.

Norman J, Olsen P and Christidis L (1998) Molecular genetics confirms taxonomic affinities of the endangered Norfolk Island Boobook Owl *Ninox novaeseelandiae undulata*. *Biological Conservation* **86**, 33–36.

Norton DA (1996) Monitoring biodiversity in New Zealand's terrestrial ecosystems. In *Papers from a Seminar Series on Biodiversity*. (Eds B McFadgen and S Simpson) pp. 19–41. Department of Conservation, Wellington, New Zealand.

Oliver I, Mac Nally R and York A (2000) Identifying performance indicators of the effects of forest management on ground-active arthropod diversity using hierarchical partitioning and partial canonical correspondence analysis. *Forest Ecology and Management* **139**, 21–40.

Olsen PD (1996) Re-establishment of an endangered subspecies: the Norfolk Island Boobook Owl *Ninox novaeseelandiae undulata*. *Bird Conservation International* **6**, 63–80.

Orians GH (1986) The place of science in environmental problem-solving. *Environment* **28**, 12–17, 38–41.

Oster M, Persson K and Eriksson O (2008) Validation of plant diversity indicators in semi-natural grasslands. *Agriculture Ecosystems and Environment* **125**, 65–72.

Paavo B, Ziegelmeyer A, Lavric E and Probert PK (2008) Morphometric correlations and body mass regression for Armandia maculata, Aglaophamus macroura (Polychaeta) and Zethalia zelandica (Gastropoda). *New Zealand Journal of Marine and Freshwater Research* **42**, 85–91.

Palo A, Linder M, Truu J and Mander U (2008) The influence of biophysical factors and former land use on forest floristic variability on Saaremaa and Muhu islands, Estonia. *Journal of Nature Conservation* **16**, 123–134.

Parsons P (1991) Biodiversity conservation under global climatic change: the insect *Drosophila* as a biological indicator? *Global Ecology and Biogeography Letters* **1**, 77–83.

Patrick R and Palavage DM (1994) The value of species as indicators of water quality. *Proceedings of the National Academy of Sciences of the United States of America* **145**, 55–92.

Patthey P, Wirthner S, Signorell N and Arlettaz R (2008) Impact of outdoor winter sports on the abundance of a key indicator species of alpine ecosystems. *Journal of Applied Ecology* **45**, 1704–1711.

Pearce J and Venier L (2005) Small mammals as bioindicators of sustainable forest management. *Forest Ecology and Management* **208**, 153–175.

Pearman PB and Weber D (2007) Common species determine richness patterns in biodiversity indicator taxa. *Biological Conservation* **138**, 109–119.

Pellet J and Schmidt BR (2005) Monitoring distribution using call surveys: estimating occupancy, detection probabilities and inferring absence. *Biological Conservation* **123**, 27–35.

Pereira HM and Cooper HD (2006) Towards the global monitoring of biodiversity change. *Trends in Ecology and Evolution* **21**, 123–129.

Pharo EJ, Beattie AJ and Binns D (1999) Vascular plant diversity as a surrogate for bryophyte and lichen diversity. *Conservation Biology* **13**, 282–292.

Phelps KL and Mcbee K (2009) Ecological characteristics of small mammal communities at a superfund site. *American Midland Naturalist* **161**, 57–68.

Plenet S (1995) Freshwater amphipods as biomonitors of metal pollution in surface and interstital systems. *Freshwater Biology* **33**, 127–137.

Ponader KC and Charles DF (2007) Diatom-based TP and TN inference models and indices for monitoring nutrient enrichment of New Jersey streams. *Ecological Indicators* **7**, 79–93.

Potapova M and Charles DF (2007) Diatom metrics for monitoring eutrophication in rivers of the United States. *Ecological Indicators* **7**, 48–70.

Reed JM and Blaustein AR (1995) Assessment of 'nondeclining' amphibian populations using power analysis. *Conservation Biology* **9**, 1299–1300.

Reid MA, Tibby JC, Penny D and Gell PA (1995) The use of diatoms to assess past and present water quality. *Australian Journal of Ecology* **20**, 57–64.

Richards GC (1991) The conservation of forest bats in Australia: do we really know the problems and solutions? In *Conservation of Australia's Forest Fauna*. (Ed D Lunney) pp. 81–90. Royal Zoological Society of New South Wales, Sydney.

Roberts KA (1991) Field monitoring: confessions of an addict. In *Monitoring for Conservation and Ecology*. (Ed. FB Goldsmith) pp. 179–212. Chapman and Hall, London.

Rodriguez-Estrella R, Donazar JD and Hiraldo F (1998) Raptors as indicators of environmental change in the scrub habitat of Baja California Sur, Mexico. *Conservation Biology* **12**, 921–925.

Rodriguez JP, Pearson DL and Barrera R (1998) A test for the adequacy of bioindicator taxa: Are tiger beetles (Coleoptera: Cicindelidae) appropriate indicators for monitoring the degradation of tropical forests in Venezuela? *Biological Conservation* **83**, 69–76.

Rogers PC and Tryel RJ (2008) Lichen community change in response to succession in Aspen forests of the southern Rocky Mountains. *Forest Ecology and Management* **256**, 1760–1770.

Rolstad J, Gjerdde I, Gundersen VS and Saetersal M (2002) Use of indicator species to assess forest continuity: a critique. *Conservation Biology* **16**, 253–257.

Rosenberry DO, Winter TC, Buso DC and Likens GE (2007) Comparison of 15 evaporation methods applied to a small mountain lake in the northeastern USA. *Journal of Hydrology* **340**, 149–166.

Roth T and Weber D (2008) Top predators as indicators for species richness? Prey species are just as useful. *Journal of Applied Ecology* **45**, 987–911.

Russell-Smith J, Whitehead PJ, Cook GD and Hoare JL (2003) Response of *Eucalyptus*-dominated savanna to frequent fires: lessons from Munmarlary 1973–1996. *Ecological Monographs* **73**, 349–375.

Sakchoowong W, Nimura S, Ogata K and Chanpaisaeng J (2008) Doversity of pselaphine beetles (Coleoptera: Staphylinidae: Pselaphinae) in eastern Thailand. *Entomological Science* **11**, 301–313.

Sato M and Riddiford N (2008) A preliminary study of the Odonata of S'Albufera Natural Park, Mallorca: status, conservation status and bio-indicator potential. *Journal of Insect Conservation* **12**, 539–548.

Scanes P (1996) 'Oyster watch': Monitoring trace metals and organochlorine concentrations in Sydney's coastal waters. *Marine Pollution Bulletin* **33**, 226–238.

Scharenberg W (1991) Cormorants *Phalacrocorax carbo sinensis* as bioindicators for polychlorinated biphenyls. *Archives of Environmental Contamination and Toxicology* **21**, 536–540.

Schelske CL and Stoermer EF (1971) Eutrophication, silica depletion, and predicted changes in algal quality in Lake Michigan. *Science* **173**, 423–424.

Schelske CL, Stoermer EF, Conley DJ, Robbins JA and Glover RM (1983) Early eutrophication in the lower Great Lakes; new evidence from biogenic silica in sediments. *Science* **222**, 320–322.

Schindler DW, Mills KH, Malley DF, Findlay DL, Shearer JA, Davies IJ, Turner MA, Linsey GA and Cruikshank DR (1985) Long-term ecosystem stress: the effects of years of experimental acidification on a small lake. *Science* **228**, 1395–1401.

Sebastiao H and Grelle CE (2009) Taxon surrogates among Amazonian mammals: Can total richness be predicted by single orders? . *Ecological Indicators* **9**, 160–166.

Sergio F, Caro T, Brown D, Clucas B, Hunter J, Ketchum J, McHugh K and Hiraldo F (2008) Top predators as conservation tools: ecological rationale, assumptions and efficacy. *Annual Review of Ecology, Evolution and Systematics* **39**, 1–19.

Shapiro J and Swain EB (1983) Lessons from the silica 'decline' in Lake Michigan. *Science* **221**, 457–459.

Sparrow HR, Sisk TD, Ehrlich PR and Murphy DD (1994) Techniques and guidelines for monitoring neotropical butterflies. *Conservation Biology* **8**, 800–809.

Spellerberg IF (1994) *Monitoring Ecological Change*. Second edition. Cambridge University Press, Cambridge.

Stankey GH, Bormann BT, Ryan C, Shindler B, Sturtevant V, Clark RN and Philpot C (2003) Adaptive management and the Northwest Forest Plan – rhetoric and reality. *Journal of Forestry* **101**, 40–46.

State of the Environment Report (2001) Biodiversity. Commonwealth of Australia, Canberra.

Stohlgren TJ, Binkley D, Veblen TT and Baker WL (1995) Attributes of reliable long-term landscape-scale studies: malpractice insurance for landscape ecologists. *Environmental Monitoring and Assessment* **36**, 1–25.

Strayer DL (1999) Statistical power of presence-absence data to detect population deciles. *Conservation Biology* **13**, 1034–1038.

Strayer DL (2008) *Freshwater Mussel Ecology: A Multifactor Approach to Distribution and Abundance*. University of California Press.

Strayer DL, Glitzenstein JS, Jones C, Kolasa J, Likens GE, McDonnell M, Parker GG and Pickett STA (1986) Long-term ecological studies: An illustrated account of their design, operation, and importance to ecology. Institute of Ecosystem Studies, Millbrook, New York.

Summerville KS, Ritter LM and Crist TO (2004) Forest moth taxa as indicators of lepidopteran richness and habitat disturbance: a preliminary assessment. *Biological Conservation* **116**, 9–18.

Suter W, Graf RF and Hess R (2002) Capercaillie (*Tetrao urogallus*) and avian biodiversity: testing the umbrella-species concept. *Conservation Biology* **16**, 778–788.

Sydes M (1994) Orchids: Indicators of management success. *Victorian Naturalist* **111**, 213–217.

Taylor B, Kremsater L and Ellis R (1998) Adaptive management of forests in British Columbia. British Columbia Ministry of Forests – Forest Practices Branch, Victoria, British Columbia.

Temple SA and Wiens JA (1989) Bird populations and environmental changes: can birds be bio-indicators? *American Birds* **43**, 260–270.

The Heinz Center (2008) The State of the Nation's Ecosystems 2008. The H. John Heinz III Center for Science, Economics and the Environment and Island Press, Washington, D.C.

Thiollay JM (1996) Rain forest communities in Sumatra: the conservation value of traditional agroforests. In *Raptors in Human Landscapes*. (Eds DM Bird, D Varland and JJ Negro) pp. 245–261. Academic Press, London.

Thompson SA, Thompson GG and Withers PC (2008) Rehabilitation index for evaluating restoration of terrestrail ecosystems using the reptile assemblage as the bioindicator. *Ecological Indicators* **8**, 530–549.

Torres MA, Barros MP, Campos SC, Pinto E, Rajamani S, Sayre RT and Colepicolo P (2008) Biochemical biomarkers in algae and marine pollution: a review. *Ecotoxicology and Environmental Safety* **71**, 1–15.

Tse P, Souissi S, Hwang J, Chen QC and Wong CK (2008) Spatial and seasonal variations in chaetognath assemblages in two subtropical marine inlets with different hydrographical characteristics. *Zoological Studies* **47**, 258–267.

Turner MG, Romme WH and Tinker DB (2003) Surprises and lessons from the 1988 Yellowstone fires. *Frontiers in Ecology and Environment* **1**, 351–358.

Underwood EC and Fischer BL (2006) The role of ants in conservation monitoring: if, how and when. *Biological Conservation* **132**, 166–182.

Wakelin J and Hill TR (2007) The impact of land transformation on breeding Blue Swallows Hirundo atrocaerulea Sundevall, in Kwazulu-Natal, South Africa. *Journal for Nature Conservation* **15**, 245–255.

Walker JF, Miller OK and Horton JL (2008) Seasonal dynamics of ectomycorrhizal fungus assemblages on oak seedlings in the southeastern Appalachian Mountains. *Mycorrhiza* **18**, 123–132.

Walker KF (1981) Ecology of freshwater mussels in the River Murray. Australian Government Publishing Service, Canberra.

Walsh PD and White LJ (1999) What it will take to monitor forest elephant populations. *Conservation Biology* **13**, 1194–1202.

Walters C (1992) Study designs for biodiversity monitoring and research. In *Methodology for Monitoring Wildlife Diversity in B.C. Forests. Proceedings of a Workshop*. (Ed. L Ramsay) pp. 1–5. British Columbia Environment, Surrey, British Columbia.

Wang DL, Miao XS and Li QX (2008) Analysis of organochlorine pesticides in coral (Porites evermanni) samples using accelerated solvent extraction and gas chromatography/ion mass spectrometry. *Archives of Environmental Contamination and Toxicology* **54**, 211–18.

Ward RC, Loftis JC and McBride GB (1986) The 'data-rich but information-poor' syndrome in water quality monitoring. *Environmental Management* **10**, 291–297.

Watson I and Novelly P (2004) Making the biodiversity monitoring system sustainable: Design issues for large-scale monitoring systems. *Austral Ecology* **29**, 16–30.

Weller MW (1995) Use of two waterbird guilds as evaluation tools for Kissimmee River restoration. *Restoration Ecology* **3**, 211–224.

Welsh AH, Cunningham RB and Chambers RL (2000) Methodology for estimating the abundance of rare animals: seabird nesting on North East Herald Cay. *Biometrics* **56**, 22–30.

Welsh HH and Ollivier LM (1998) Stream amphibians as indicators of ecosystem stress: a case study from California's redwoods *Ecological Applications* **8**, 1118–1132.

Whelan RJ (1995) *The Ecology of Fire*. Cambridge University Press, Cambridge.

Wolseley PA and Aguirre-Hudson B (1991) Lichens as indicators of environmental change in the tropical forests of Thailand. *Global Ecology and Biogeography Letters* **1**, 170–175.

Woodward A, Jenkins K and Schreiner EG (1999) The role of ecological theory in long-term monitoring: Report on a workshop. *Natural Areas Journal* **19**, 223–233.

Wright-Stow AE and Winterbourn MJ (2003) How well do New Zealand's stream-monitoring indicators, the Macroinvertebrate Community Index and its quantitative variant, correspond? *New Zealand Journal of Marine and Freshwater Research* **37**, 461–470.

Wu RS and Lau TC (1996) Polymer-ligands: A novel chemical device for monitoring heavy metals in aquatic environments. *Marine Pollution Bulletin* **32**, 391–396.

Yoccoz NG, Nichols JD and Boulinier T (2001) Monitoring of biological diversity in space and time. *Trends in Ecology and Evolution* **16**, 446–453.

Zeide B (1994) Big projects, big problems. *Environmental Monitoring and Assessment* **33**, 115–133.

Zhan X, Li MY, Zhang Z, Goossens B, Chen Y, Wang H, Bruford M and Wei F (2006) Molecular censusing doubles giant panda population estimate in a key nature reserve. *Current Biology* **16**, R451–452.

Zochler C, Miles L, Fish L, Wolf A, Rees G and Danks F (2008) Potential impact of climate change and reindeer density on tundra indicator species in the Barents Sea region. *Climate Change* **87**, 119–130.

Chapter 3

What makes effective
long-term monitoring?

In Chapter 2 we outlined some of the characteristics of ineffective monitoring programs and highlighted why some fail or are unsuccessful. As an antidote to that rather depressing discussion, in this chapter we describe the characteristics of effective and successful monitoring programs. We then outline a new paradigm – Adaptive Monitoring – which collects together many of these characteristics in a broad framework to guide successful monitoring programs (Lindenmayer and Likens 2009). Many of the attributes of successful monitoring programs will be apparent in the examples of successful case studies that appear in Chapter 4. Ecologists, like all scientists, learn by doing (Walters and Holling 1990) and that is the theme of the next two chapters.

CHARACTERISTICS OF EFFECTIVE MONITORING PROGRAMS

If we ask, what are the key characteristics of effective monitoring programs?, we can isolate what appear to be key points, but we should be mindful that the keys to success are all strongly interrelated.

There are several ways of gaining long-term information, including empirical or natural history studies; retrospective studies; modelling studies; space-for-time studies; experimental manipulation studies, and direct long-term monitoring (Likens 1989; Likens 1992). Each of these approaches can provide important insights into how systems work, but a combination of these approaches is even more powerful, giving a more integrated and synthetic view of long-term phenomena. Cost, expertise and time often limit the use of multiple approaches, but multiple approaches should remain a goal, even when it is not always possible to achieve this integration.

Long-term records of ecological phenomena are rare and difficult to obtain, but they provide unique insights into how an ecosystem works (Chapter 1). As such, these records are a critical component of overall ecological inquiry (e.g. Likens 1989; Likens 1992; Carpenter 1998; Nichols and Williams 2006; Lovett *et al.* 2007; Krebs *et al.* 2008). Long-term records are usually developed through monitoring of ecosystem parameters (optimally guided by questions, not mindless collection of data).

The integrity and application of quality assurance/quality control protocols are pivotal to the success of long-term research (see Buso *et al.* 2000; Hirsch *et al.* 2006; Lovett *et al.* 2007). Without high quality assurance/quality control, long-term records can be seriously compromised.

Exemplary examples of monitoring include the pioneering efforts at Rothamsted, England (see Chapter 4), the US Weather Service, the US Geological Survey, and British Breeding Bird Survey. FLUXNET is a global network of micrometeorological towers focused on carbon dioxide fluxes (e.g. EUROFLUX, AmeriFlux, AsiaFlux, MEDEFLU and OzNet networks). In the last three decades in the USA, there have been major attempts to initiate and sustain long-term research and monitoring. Examples include Long-Term Research in Environmental Biology (LTREB); Long-Term Ecological Research (LTER) – although LTREB and LTER are not monitoring networks *per se*; Atmospheric Integrated Research Monitoring Network (AIRMoN); Clean Air Status and Trends Network (CASTNeT); Canadian Air and Precipitation Monitoring Network (CAPMoN); US Forest Inventory Analysis (FIA), and the Temporally Integrated Monitoring of Ecosystems (TIME) programs. In spite of the documented value of such efforts (Likens 1989), they often are supported by fickle finances, and thus are difficult to maintain over the truly long term.

Good questions and evolving questions

Posing good questions lies at the heart of good science and hence is essential to effective monitoring (Nichols and Williams 2006). This is a far from trivial task – '*90% of a problem is often defining the problem*'. Some authors argue that ecologists and resource managers have been poor at problem definition and objective setting (Peters 1991). This is perhaps not surprising because it is very difficult to pose good questions. Indeed, some Nobel Prize winners believe they have developed only two or three really good questions in their entire career! Good-question setting must result in quantifiable objectives that offer unambiguous signposts for measuring progress (Lindenmayer *et al.* 2007). As outlined further below, setting good questions requires a well-developed partnership among scientists, statisticians, resource managers and policy-makers (Gibbons *et al.* 2008). Thus, good questions must be scientifically tractable and test real policy and resource management options (Walters 1986).

For a wide range of reasons, the key questions being addressed in a project may change or evolve during a long-term study or monitoring program. This is challenging because it requires a nimble approach to allow these changes to be made when required (Ringold *et al.* 1996), but without breaching the integrity of the overall monitoring program (Lindenmayer and Likens 2009). As an example, the long-term monitoring program for arboreal marsupials in the wet forests of Victoria (south-eastern Australia) was initially focused on the endangered species Leadbeater's possum (Lindenmayer *et al.* 2003). Although this is a high profile species of conservation concern, it is also relatively rare and it can be difficult to gather large quantities of data on it. After the monitoring program for the species had commenced, officials from the Victorian State Government requested that the focus of work be altered to include the abundance of all species. A rotating, site-selection process was sufficiently flexible to enable this suggested change to be accommodated (Lindenmayer *et al.* 2003). In more recent years, newly recruited staff in the Victorian State Government requested the focus of the monitoring program be returned to Leadbeater's possum, in part because of demands of the State of Victoria's Recovery Plan for the species. Again, the statistical methodology employed to guide site selection and survey allowed this change in focus to take place without breaching the integrity of the overall monitoring program (see Chapter 4). Importantly, the monitoring program was carefully focused on Leadbeater's possum and other species of arboreal marsupials and sought to answer key questions about the population dynamics of these species. At no stage was it ever assumed that Leadbeater's possum nor any other species were valid 'indicator species' (Lindenmayer and Cunningham 1997) (see Chapter 2). Finally, in 2009, major fires demanded yet further changes to the long-term monitoring program in which new questions were posed as part of quantifying post-fire ecological recovery and accordingly the rotating-site sampling strategy had to accommodate comparisons of burned and unburned sites.

The use of a conceptual model

A conceptual model of the ecosystem or particular entity to be targeted for monitoring is one way to help guide the development of the question(s) to be addressed (Woodward *et al.* 1999). Such a model can guide the development of *a priori* predictions about how an ecosystem or other kind of entity (e.g. a population of a species) might behave, for example, in response to a human intervention (e.g. clearcutting of a catchment or prescribed burning of a patch). A conceptual model, developed at the beginning of a study, forces the collection together of ideas to formulate theory about how an ecosystem or target entity works, and helps to ensure that all the relevant components are captured in the project design.

A conceptual model needs to capture the inputs and outputs for an ecosystem and thereby show the connections of that particular ecosystem with the remainder of the biosphere. These abiotic and biotic inputs and outputs then highlight the critical attributes of the ecosystem that need to be managed. These inputs and outputs identify the clear targets for management of environmental problems (see case studies in Chapter 4)

By understanding the input and outputs within the framework of conceptual model, it is then possible to understand the mechanisms for change in an ecosystem and what responses might occur as a consequence of management interventions. This approach creates a powerful capability for making informed predictions and subsequently testing them as part of ecosystem management.

A conceptual model needs to be able to guide continued and ongoing research and thinking. It becomes a focal point for discussions among partners – scientists, managers and policy-makers – about how an ecosystem might be managed or protected. Such discussions are particularly important when dealing with complex natural systems and bringing people together to generate a common view about an appropriate way forward.

Conceptual models can fail to guide long-term research and monitoring when they are either too detailed (the 'devil is in the details'), too abstract or vague, or unsuitable for answering specific or new questions (like having the wrong vessel in a laboratory experiment), or not being particularly pertinent to the research site. Many such conceptual models fail to guide research or be used, particularly regarding adaptive monitoring issues, in long-term studies.

We show in Figures 3.1 and 3.2 conceptual models of the dynamics of coarse woody debris in the wet forests of Tasmania. They were developed to guide a series of major studies that are taking place at the Warra Long-term Ecological Research site (Grove 2007). The models are quite complex. As we discuss in Chapter 4, conceptual models are often most useful for developing tractable questions and subsequent long-term studies if they are relatively simple. An example of a more simple and tractable conceptual model is the one that has been used successfully for decades to guide thinking and

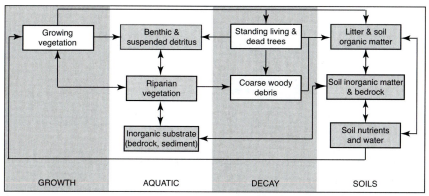

Figure 3.1 The conceptual model for guiding research at Warra Long-term Ecological Research site in southern Tasmania. (Redrawn from Grove 2007)

research for the Hubbard Brook Ecosystem Study in the White Mountains of New Hampshire, USA (Bormann and Likens 1967) (Figure 4.10).

Selection of appropriate entities to measure

Progress in many monitoring programs is hamstrung by wrangles over what to monitor. We highlighted in Chapter 2 two approaches that are commonly but often unsuccessfully employed to tackle this problem. These were attempts to monitor (almost) 'everything' or to monitor so-called indicator species thought to be surrogates for other entities (e.g. effects of a pollutant; see Spellerberg 1994) or for other groups of biota or ecosystem processes (reviewed by Landres *et al.* 1988; Lindenmayer *et al.* 2000).

We believe that the problems of 'laundry lists' and indicator species can be avoided by carefully crafting questions at the onset of a monitoring program, using a well-conceived model to help conceptualise a particular ecosystem and make predictions about ecosystem behavior and response (see above). These key steps will help identify those entities most appropriate for monitoring. Such a focused scientific approach obviates the need to measure a vast array of things and ensures that a subset of entities can be monitored well, rather than vice-versa. In addition, making direct measures of targeted entities avoids the need to assume that those entities are surrogates or indicators of other entities.

Good design

A monitoring program can be based on excellent questions that are developed using a conceptual model and well focused on an appropriate set of attributes to measure, but still fail when it is poorly designed. Good statistical design is a critical component of any successful monitoring program.

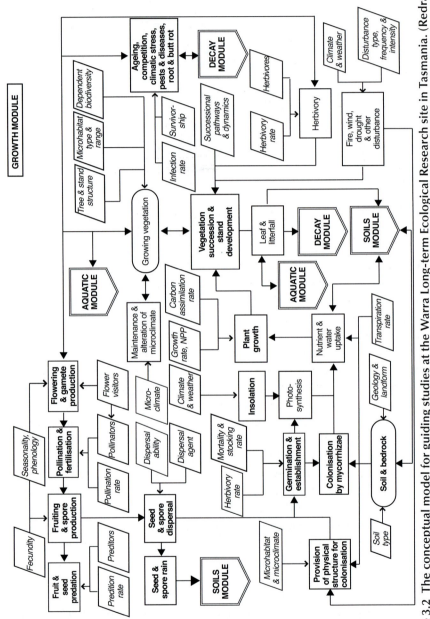

Figure 3.2 The conceptual model for guiding studies at the Warra Long-term Ecological Research site in Tasmania. (Redrawn from Grove 2007)

Martin *et al.* (2007) correctly believe that proponents of monitoring programs should spend more time getting their study design right. For example, some of the strongest designs to guide a monitoring program will often be those where there are contrasting management interventions that enable strong inferences to be made about both how and why an ecosystem or other entity like a population has changed either spatially, temporally, or spatio-temporally.

We believe that professional statistical advice should be at the core of most of the key phases of a monitoring program. This recommendation is made because good study design is an inherently statistical process (Field *et al.* 2007) and many key approaches to experimental design and the analysis of environmental data are not those which many scientists, resource managers and policy-makers will find readily accessible.

Good study design is invariably linked with expert statistical analyses of data once data are gathered. In fact, the analysis and interpretation of results from monitoring programs can be extremely challenging (Thomas and Martin 1996; Welsh *et al.* 2000; Nichols and Williams 2006). For example, separating long-term population declines from annual or cyclical fluctuations in population size is a non-trivial task (Krebs 1991; Thomas and Martin 1996; Sauer *et al.* 1998; Martin *et al.* 2007). This task is particularly true for some rare species for which it may be difficult to determine if they are declining (Taylor and Gerrodette 1993; Martin *et al.* 2007) or for populations of species which can exhibit rapid short-term fluctuations in population size such as after disturbances like logging (Loyn 1985; Brawn *et al.* 2001) or fire (Whelan 1995; Bradstock *et al.* 2002; Lindenmayer *et al.* 2008).

The challenges of good design, coupled with the rigor of subsequent statistical analyses of high-quality environmental data, emphasise the fact that monitoring programs can be (and should be) good science (Nichols and Williams 2006; Lindenmayer and Likens 2009). Conquering these challenges means that the distinction between research and monitoring also should be blurred (Franklin *et al.* 1999). As noted by Walters (1997), researchers should be attracted to the prospect of conducting large scale, well-designed and replicated monitoring studies of direct relevance to natural resource management.

Well-developed partnerships

The previous section emphasised the role of statistical science in the experimental design, data analysis and data interpretation phases of monitoring programs. Most successful monitoring programs are built on partnerships between people with different but complementary sets of skills (Hong and

BOX 3.1 A NOVEL AND NON-STANDARD OVERLAPPING AND ROTATING STATISTICAL DESIGN FOR INCREASING INFERENCE FROM MONITORING PROGRAMS

The majority of monitoring programs are based on traditional visit–revisit protocols. That is, a specified number of sites is visited at a given frequency (e.g. annually). However, this design can be limiting if it is difficult to measure more than a small number of sites during any given time interval (e.g. a field season). This limitation is the case for a major long-term monitoring program of arboreal marsupials in the wet forests of Victoria in Australia. For that work, all large trees on a given 1 hectare (ha) site must be watched simultaneously at dusk by well-trained volunteers to generate an accurate count of the numbers of each species of arboreal marsupial on that site (Lindenmayer *et al.* 1991). This is a time-consuming and labor-intensive method, but no others provide counts with an appropriate level of accuracy (Smith *et al.* 1989). Weather conditions, logistical factors and financial constraints mean that no more than 40 sites can typically be surveyed in any given year. A monitoring study of 40 sites would be limited to a subset of the environmental conditions relevant to arboreal marsupials in the study area. Hence, levels of inference from the study would be restrictive.

A novel and non-standard overlapping and rotating statistical design was adapted from a long-term monitoring program of seabirds in the Coral Sea and used to solve the problems for the monitoring program in the wet forests of Victoria. The monitoring program was based on a retrospective approach to re-survey populations of arboreal marsupials on sites first surveyed in 1983. A pool of 161 sites was established and each site has a history of repeated field surveys over the past two decades. All 161 sites were re-surveyed in 1997–1998 and a randomly selected subset of between 30 and 40 of the 161 sites has been re-sampled for animals between 1999 and 2008 (Lindenmayer *et al.* 2003). The probability of site selection was based on the count of the number of animals recorded on those sites in the previous surveys, including the census year in 1997. Overall, the monitoring design allowed for approximately 80% of all sampled sites to remain the same from one year to the following year with an emphasis on counts on sites with high numbers of animals, but sites with few animals typically being surveyed every three to four years (Lindenmayer *et al.* 2003).

The monitoring program has been specifically designed to provide strong statistical inferences about population trends in arboreal marsupials. Year-to-year partial sampling has allowed short-term temporal fluctuations in population dynamics to be separated from long-term trends such as population declines (Welsh *et al.* 2000). A key advantage of the non-standard overlapping and rotating sampling approach was that it enabled a far greater number and range of sites to be included in the monitoring program (see below) than if a traditional annual sample and resample method were used. This approach greatly broadened the kinds of inferences that could be made from the monitoring program. The statistical advantages of non-standard, overlapping, rotating designs for monitoring programs are further discussed by Welsh *et al.* (2000).

Page 2004). These include scientists, statisticians, policy-makers and resource managers who may be from government and non-government organisations, universities, research institutions and other organisations. Well-developed partnerships between these groups of people are needed to make sure that policy-relevant and management-relevant projects are undertaken, but with the scientific and statistical rigor required that ensure results are robust and that conclusions are defensible. Ludwig *et al.* (2001) even contend that although scientists are good at identifying problems, they are often not good at solving the policy-implementation component of these problems. In contrast, policy professionals are frequently better equipped to find tractable solutions. Thus, the need for these diverse groups to work together to find workable solutions to environmental problems is clear.

Partnerships are important for other reasons. They can facilitate the flow of information between parties in ways that people from different backgrounds and with different expertise can readily understand. In other cases, particular agencies may no longer maintain the expertise and capability to do long-term monitoring (see Chapter 5).

True collaborative partnerships are also essential because policy-makers and resource managers will often not know how to frame questions in ways that can be resolved by well–executed monitoring, or may initially pose too many questions without prioritising them. They also may have unreasonable expectations about what questions or problems can and cannot be solved by scientific projects and how much effective monitoring costs. Thus, policy-makers need to understand better the scientific approach and the importance of posing the right questions and in the correct way (see Chapter 2). Conversely, scientists need to articulate better what kinds of questions they can and cannot answer. They also need to understand better the complexity of the policy process (Clark 2002; Pielke 2007). Scientists will often not fully comprehend the kinds of key problems faced by policy-makers and resource managers that need to be addressed by long-term research and monitoring (Russell-Smith *et al.* 2003). Nor will scientists necessarily be fully aware of the policy options and the range of on-ground management interventions available for testing and monitoring

BOX 3.2 TESTS OF MANAGEMENT RELEVANCE - THE IMPACTS OF ACID RAIN ON TERRESTRIAL AND AQUATIC ECOSYSTEMS IN THE HUBBARD BROOK VALLEY

Effective monitoring programs are those that pass the test of management relevance (Russell-Smith et al. 2003). Monitoring, understanding and then mitigating the effects of acid rain illustrates this interaction.

The very first sample of rain collected in July of 1963, as part of the Hubbard Brook Ecosystem Study in the White Mountains of New Hampshire (www.hubbardbrook.org), was surprisingly acid (pH 3.7). But it took decades of monitoring and study to understand the numerous connections between atmospheric emissions, deposition and ecological response in recipient terrestrial and aquatic ecosystems. Long-term data on precipitation chemistry were critical to the debate and ultimate passage of the 1990 Amendments to the Clean Air Act in the USA. They also stimulated many new scientific studies and raised awareness about the effects of human activities on natural ecosystems.

An important finding from these long-term studies was that both atmospheric deposition and streamwater concentrations and output of SO_4^{2-} at the Hubbard Brook Experimental Forest were significantly correlated with emissions of SO_2 from the emission source area for the Hubbard Brook Experimental Forest. Like SO_4^{2-}, atmospheric deposition of NO_3^- at the Hubbard Brook Experimental Forest is correlated with NO_x emissions (Butler et al. 2001; Butler et al. 2003). Determining whether these critical relationships will become more robust or weaker as emissions of SO_2 and NO_x decrease in response to the 1990 Clean Air Act Amendments is an active area of inquiry addressed by long-term monitoring at the site.

The causes, distribution and ecological effects of acid rain have been studied and debated in North America since 1972 (Likens et al. 1972; Likens and Bormann 1974; Likens et al. 1979; Schindler et al. 1985; Charles 1991; Driscoll et al. 2001; Likens et al. 2001; Weathers et al. 2009). The Hubbard Brook Experimental Forest is an important site for monitoring atmospheric pollutants in the north-eastern USA because of the long record, location 'downwind' of major emission sources and lack of large, local pollution sources.

Acid rain continues to have major environmental impact on terrestrial and aquatic ecosystems of the Hubbard Brook Experimental Forest in spite of decreases in emissions of sulphur dioxide and nitrous oxides from the emission source area during the past several years (Likens et al. 2002; Likens 2004). Given the cost and angst involved with federal legislation to reduce emissions of the major acid rain precursors, sulphur dioxide and nitrous oxides, it is important to continue long-term measurement of acid rain and its impact on

> recipient forest and aquatic ecosystems that now have become increasingly sensitive to these acidic inputs (Likens *et al.* 1996; Likens *et al.* 2001; Likens 2004; Likens and Franklin 2009).

in a particular ecosystem (Walters 1986). Thus, without guidance, scientists may implement long-term research and monitoring programs that answer questions with limited value for informing specific management actions. As we outlined earlier, professional statistical advice is essential to ensure that an appropriate experimental design can be developed to answer rigorously the questions conjointly conceived by scientists, policy-makers and resource managers.

Developing partnerships is a challenge because representatives of different groups speak different 'languages', have different work cultures, different reward systems and different skill sets (Gibbons *et al.* 2008). Trust and mutual respect is essential, in part because various kinds of knowledge – scientific, policy and political knowledge – together influence decision-making in natural resource management (Pielke 2007). Hence, for example, good science alone is insufficient as it often will need to be translated into a form that policy-makers and resource managers can understand and use (King 2004).

Strong and dedicated leadership

Strong, dedicated and focused leadership is essential to almost all effective monitoring programs – someone with 'fire-in-the-belly' to keep the work going (Strayer *et al.* 1986; Norton 1996; Lovett *et al.* 2007). In many cases, long-term projects and team leaders even become synonymous (Strayer *et al.* 1986). Effective leadership is pivotal to all of the fundamental characteristics of successful monitoring programs described earlier in this Chapter – setting appropriate questions, identifying new questions, developing a workable conceptual model, resolving suitable entities to measure, guiding study design, analysing data, communicating results to management agencies, policy makers and the public, and establishing and maintaining partnerships. Leadership is also critical to many other factors that are discussed below, such as securing funding and ensuring good project management, both of which contribute to effective long-term monitoring programs. Leadership embodies both scientific and management leadership, as most successful long-term programs have a champion within a management agency. Indeed, partnerships appear to work best when there is a problem with a shared responsibility to find a solution. Major

BOX 3.3 LARGE MAMMALIAN HERBIVORE–ECOSYSTEM INTERACTIONS: A CASE STUDY FROM THE BOREAL FORESTS OF ISLE ROYALE

John Pastor
Department of Biology
University of Minnesota
Duluth, Minnesota

Large mammalian herbivores have long generation times and range over large portions of the landscape. Their foraging can greatly change species composition, net primary productivity, litterfall, and soil nitrogen availability over long periods and large areas of the landscape (Danell *et al.* 2006). Elucidating these long-term and large-scale processes requires comparable long-term, systematic experiments and monitoring designed to test hypotheses specifically focused at these large and long scales.

Moose are one of the major herbivores of boreal forests worldwide. A single adult moose requires approximately 10 kilograms of dry matter per day. Moose therefore have considerable potential to control boreal ecosystems through their foraging decisions. Our original hypothesis was that by foraging on small-diameter aspen (*Populus tremuloides)* and birch *(Betula papyrifera)* whose leaves and twigs have high nitrogen and low lignin contents, moose convert boreal forests more quickly to dominance by unpreferred spruce (*Picea glauca)* and balsam fir (*Abies balsamea)* with low nitrogen, high lignin and high phenolic contents. These same chemical properties determine decay and nitrogen release rates of litter. We therefore predicted that productivity and nitrogen cycling would decrease as moose foraging increases dominance by conifers. Clearly, these effects of moose may require decades to take effect.

Fortunately, some long-term experiments can be found ready-made. Yosef Cohen and I and our graduate students Ron Moen and Pam McInnes began our work by taking advantage of several long-term moose exclosures on Isle Royale established by Laurits Krefting of the University of Minnesota St Paul in the late 1940s. Krefting had already established that aspen, birch and other preferred species remained dominant inside the exclosures while the vegetation outside the exclosures became increasingly dominated by the less preferred spruce and fir. If our hypothesis was correct, litterfall should be more dominated by conifer litter and net primary productivity, microbial biomass and nitrogen mineralisation rates should be lower in control plots than in the exclosures. These predictions were confirmed by McInnes *et al.* (1992) and Pastor *et al.* (1988; 1993). Newer long-term exclosure experiments established in northern Sweden extend these results beyond Isle Royale to Scandinavia (Persson *et al.* 2005; Persson *et al.* 2009).

As clear as these experimental results were, they raised more questions. How common are these results over the entire landscape? Are the effects of moose overridden by topography, bedrock, disturbances and other factors? Are these effects randomly distributed across the landscape or is there some spatial pattern to them? To answer these questions we began a second phase to our long-term program by monitoring the spatial distribution and dynamics of moose browsing intensity, plant species composition and soil nitrogen availability in two, 6-ha grids of 100 points apiece at an average spacing of 24 metres in two valleys on Isle Royale for the past 18 years. We initially found that the spatial distribution of these properties is not random but instead distributed in waveform patterns (Pastor *et al.* 1998). These waveform patterns do not correspond to topography, bedrock geology, fire history or any other conceivable cause other than the effects of the moose population. They also resemble similar waveform patterns in reaction-diffusion models of a predator (in this case, the moose) and its prey (i.e., the two plant species). Over the 18 years of monitoring, the spatial distributions of moose browsing and its effects on plants and soil nitrogen availability have changed in response to moose population cycles. The waveform distribution was most clearly expressed when moose population densities were at their peak, but when moose population densities crashed to historically low levels, the distribution of browsing and its effects became more random (De Jager and Pastor 2009; DeJager *et al.* 2009).

Long-term monitoring has demonstrated that moose exert a great deal of control of plant species composition, net primary productivity, litterfall and soil nitrogen availability across boreal landscapes. The nature of this control varies with the phase of the moose population cycle. Because these cycles happen on decadal time scales, it was imperative for us to maintain a continuous monitoring program across almost two decades and that exclosures four decades old were available to us. Measurements made on shorter time scales may have been contingent on the phase of the moose population cycle in which they occurred. A full understanding of how large mammals control ecosystem processes can only emerge from long-term studies.

environmental problems provide a good example of where these partnerships are critical.

Strength of leadership, paradoxically, also can be the Achilles heel of monitoring programs. This problem occurs because many programs are prone to collapse when a leader leaves (Strayer *et al.* 1986; Norton 1996) (see Chapter 2). This problem illustrates the need for succession planning, often at an earlier stage than many senior scientists and project managers sometimes recognise.

BOX 3.4 THE IMPORTANCE OF DOING IT RIGHT

In the early 1950s, Dr Charles David Keeling, a postdoctoral atmospheric scientist at the California Institute of Technology was measuring carbon in river water and carbon dioxide in the air. He found, surprisingly, that the air had a constant value of 310 parts per million if samples were collected remotely, away from obvious sinks and sources of carbon dioxide. He then moved to the Scripps Institution of Oceanography in La Jolla, California, to work with Roger Revelle on carbon dioxide in the atmosphere. Because of prior connections with Harry Wexler of the US Weather Service, he was able to establish a monitoring station on Mauna Loa on the Island of Hawaii in the Hawaiian Island archipelago in 1958 (http://scrippsco2.ucsd.edu). There were several potential problems with this location, including that the site was close to an active volcano on the island. On the positive side, the site was above the tree line and situated to sample the easterly trade winds with no major air pollution sources upwind for thousands of kilometers. Being a thoughtful and careful scientist, Keeling set aside a large cylinder of carbon dioxide at the beginning of his study to use in calibrating his gas-measuring instruments as the study progressed. He wasn't particularly concerned that the stated concentration of carbon dioxide in the cylinder was accurate, just that it would not change over time and serve as a standard or reference to calibrate his instruments in the future to this initial value. Such standards are key to successful long-term monitoring and they can be of many types, both biotic and abiotic.

After some 10 years of careful measurements of carbon dioxide at the monitoring site on Mauna Loa, carefully 'filtering' out any contamination from upslope winds, which had passed over vegetation at lower elevations, Keeling had obtained two remarkable findings: **(1)** the concentration of carbon dioxide in the atmosphere was increasing, and, **(2)** there was a consistent, seasonal pattern of increase and decrease of carbon dioxide concentration, which Keeling attributed to global biotic processes of photosynthesis and respiration (Figure 3.4).

Also, shortly thereafter, his funding sources (the National Science Foundation (NSF) and the National Oceanographic and Atmospheric Administration (NOAA)) questioned whether these studies needed to be continued – 'Haven't we learned all we need to know from this study?' 'Isn't 20 years long enough?' One of us (GEL) was asked to join a Department of Energy (DOE) Technical Advisory Group on carbon dioxide to address this issue. The review team of 12 met at Scripps Institution of Oceanography in LaJolla, CA in 1977-78. Keeling was adamant that the study needed to continue and the review committee agreed, giving him and the monitoring program a strong endorsement to continue. At that point the Department of Energy came to his rescue with funding for continuation of the program (Figure 3.3). The rest is history, so to speak. The study did continue, as did the long-term record of carbon dioxide concentrations from Mauna Loa, arguably one of the most important environmental records in the world (Figure 3.3). These continuous and long-term data have provided the basic information about carbon dioxide increase in the world's atmosphere, which in turn has led to understandings about global warming and climate change (http://scrippsco2.ucsd.edu). Other monitoring sites throughout the world have confirmed Keeling's original findings about carbon dioxide, and the continuing long-term record (now funded and maintained at the National Oceanographic and Atmospheric Administration's Mauna Loa Observatory) establishes the baseline for evaluating ongoing changes in atmospheric chemistry, as well as providing discoveries and new scientific questions to be explored (e.g. Keeling *et al.* 1995; Keeling *et al.* 1996). Charles David Keeling died in 2005 at the age of 77, having received numerous prestigious awards for his work.

Ongoing funding

No project can proceed or be maintained without access to funding. Generating the funding to maintain long-term monitoring programs is a truly major challenge and few individuals and organisations have ever managed to do it successfully (Strayer *et al.* 1986). We discuss the many reasons for

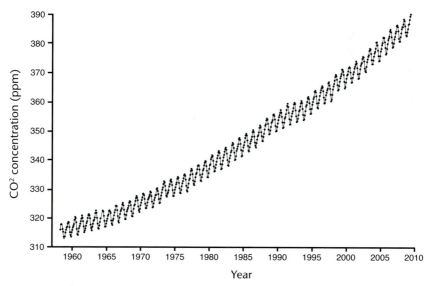

Figure 3.3 The Mauna Loa (Hawaii, USA) record of atmospheric CO_2 concentrations. (Redrawn from www.scrippsco2.ucsd.edu)

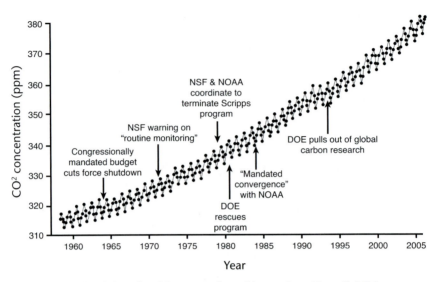

Figure 3.4 Maintaining the CO$_2$ curve from Mauna Loa, Hawaii, USA. (Redrawn from http://scrippsco2.ucsd.edu)

this challenge in Chapter 5, but suggest that many of the underlying problems appear to be associated with the culture of 'short-termism' that pervades the culture of science and the culture of western societies; cultures which are fundamentally mal-adapted to long-term work.

Successful programs where funding has been maintained are characterised by many of the factors discussed above such as strong leadership, evolving questions that are highly relevant to resource management and society's need to know, and high levels of scientific productivity (i.e. published articles, books and media reports). In some cases, successful ongoing funding is linked with appropriate matching of the size of a monitoring program with the scale of a human activity (e.g. a logging operation) (Franklin *et al.* 1999; Lindenmayer and Franklin 2002) or the overall budget for the management of a National Park or nature reserve (Edwards *et al.* 2003). In some cases (e.g. www.earthwatch.org/FieldReportpdf/Dyer_fieldreport2005.pdf) the 'fire-in-the-belly' is so strong that personal funds have been used for years to support long-term monitoring (also see Chapters 4 and 5).

Frequent use of data

Another key ingredient for maintaining long records of high quality is the frequent examination and use of these data. Such examinations result in important discoveries and stimulate new research and management questions. They are also the primary way errors, artifacts or other problems are uncovered, and enthusiasm about the research is sustained. Moreover, it is much easier to resolve a problem in long-term data when it is identified in a timely fashion and while observers and methods are still available for examination and discussion.

Scientific productivity

One criterion often used to gauge success is scientific productivity. We strongly believe that the results of monitoring programs must be published in peer-reviewed literature. This outreach is essential to inform the public, funders and resource managers about valuable findings, and it helps to establish the credibility, quality and visibility of a project. This outreach is, in turn, essential to convince funders that investments are appropriate and should be maintained. It is notable that high numbers of scientific publications have characterised all of the effective monitoring programs featured in this chapter and the following one (see Chapter 4).

A potential problem is that it takes a long time to generate long-term trends and patterns with empirical data. Hence, it can take a long time to generate substantial scientific publications from such kinds of work. This delay can be perceived as a lack of productivity and threaten the continuity of a project. As a counter to this problem, we believe there can be considerable value in exploring avenues to generate rapid returns on research and monitoring investments and hence highlight scientific productivity. A long-term monitoring program can be used as a framework around which shorter-term projects can be conducted. For example, retrospective or cross-sectional studies can serve as a prelude to longer-term projects and can provide key initial insights or questions. These other projects, often built around the major research program (including student projects), add value to overall research effort and enrich the overall body of scientific knowledge. Various kinds of collective evidence derived from several kinds of studies can strengthen an overall research effort, make a body of scientific knowledge more compelling and allow for an examination of consistency of research outcomes.

Working with the news media to generate high-quality and timely reports about long-term data, particularly about trends and extremes discovered, can be another way to enhance outreach from long-term research and monitoring programs. Such reports can be very effective in informing the public, policy-makers and funders about environmental issues and the research being done (e.g. Likens 1992).

Maintenance of data integrity and calibration of field techniques

New sensors, modified or new analytical procedures and real-time data can add significantly to long-term data (Hirsch *et al.* 2006), but offsets and glitches generated by new methodology are a common problem in long-term data sets and must be addressed carefully (see the case of population monitoring of the giant panda in Chapter 2). We return to this topic in Chapter 5. In the long-term Hubbard Brook Ecosystem Study, an analytical method or procedure is not replaced with a new one without first overlapping the two. This overlapping period may be for many months or for more than a year to compare results and avoid offsets in the record due to different methodologies (Buso *et al.* 2000). Also, many samples are stored for later analysis to help reconcile problems and to enable new questions to be pursued when new technology becomes available (e.g. see Alewell *et al.* 1999).

LITTLE THINGS MATTER A LOT! SOME 'TRICKS OF THE TRADE'

Several seemingly small factors contribute enormously to the success of long-term monitoring, sometimes out of proportion to expectations. These include (1) safe and adequate field vehicles (trucks, snowmobiles, boats, etc.); (2) continuity of field staff; (3) access to field sites, and (4) spending time in residence at field sites. We base all of these things on the assumption that long-term monitoring occurs primarily at a field site, often remote, and sometimes relatively inaccessible.

Field transport

The availability of reliable transportation to a field site is critical to maintain routine sampling protocols and especially for sampling during unusual events and on short notice, such as following a storm or a fire, where samples must be collected quickly to characterise the initial conditions following such disturbance. Waiting to obtain access to a vehicle through 'normal channels' (e.g. commercial rental or university fleet service late at night or over a weekend) could seriously compromise the integrity of a long-term record, and indeed, the scientific validity of a study. Administrators and funding agencies frequently argue that the expense for purchase and maintenance of such field vehicles is an unnecessary 'luxury'. They do not understand the critical importance of this basic infrastructural support.

Moreover, specialised field vehicles can be as important to the success of monitoring as an electron microscope or mass spectrometer are to a laboratory-orientated scientist. It is very important to be able to access field sites quickly, safely and on short notice whenever the scientifically driven need arises. Even hours of delay in collecting such samples could jeopardise the integrity and value of a long-term record. Manual sampling of storm-generated hydrographs in streams or rivers during flooding conditions is a good example.

Field staff

Maintaining motivated staff for long periods is critical to the success of long-term monitoring and pivotal to the collection of high-quality, long-term data. Dedicated, intelligent and trained staff that work for a long time on a project bring many vital intangibles to the effort, including:

- knowledge of what to do and how to do it;
- dedication to the collection of samples or data, often under arduous environmental conditions;
- ensuring the consistency of analysis (e.g. taxonomic knowledge of diverse organisms (phytoplankton or zooplankton) and thus being able to notice in a timely manner when there is a temporal change in such organisms;
- maintaining enthusiasm for the overall success of a project, and
- generating new questions that could or should be pursued as a result of spending a great deal of time in the field on a project.

Access to field sites

Access to remote field sites can be problematic because of inclement weather, poor road or boating conditions, security barriers, or potential harm to the organisms or structure of the field site (e.g. excessive disturbance by trampling during sample collection). Care and planning can help anticipate and avoid these problems and sustain the integrity of long-term records. Maintaining the infrastructure that is necessary for site access should be a high priority. Security of tenure is part of this requirement, and this includes not only the immediate field site but the surrounding landscape which could affect processes that spill over into the immediate study area (e.g. Laurance and Luizao 2007).

Time in the field

Based on our collective experience, we are convinced that it is extremely important for research personnel, including principal investigators, to spend significant amounts of time working together at long-term monitoring sites. Numerous examples exist where increased idea generation and novel and profound research initiatives have been generated from the melting pot of senior and junior scientists spending significant time working together at field sites (e.g. see also Chapter 2; Stokstad 2008). We further discuss problems associated with a lack of time in the field in Chapter 5.

THE ADAPTIVE MONITORING FRAMEWORK

Based on some of the salient features that should accompany effective monitoring programs, we propose a new approach to monitoring programs, which encompasses these features. We term this paradigm 'Adaptive Monitoring' and show its key steps in Figure 3.5. We recognise that many other authors have recommended changes to overcome the deficiencies of existing monitoring programs (e.g. Yoccoz *et al.* 2001; Nichols and Williams 2006; Field *et al.* 2007), but we have not seen a framework proposed within which to do this effectively (Lindenmayer and Likens 2009).

The Adaptive Monitoring framework is motivated by questions carefully posed at the outset. In fact, we strongly believe that effective

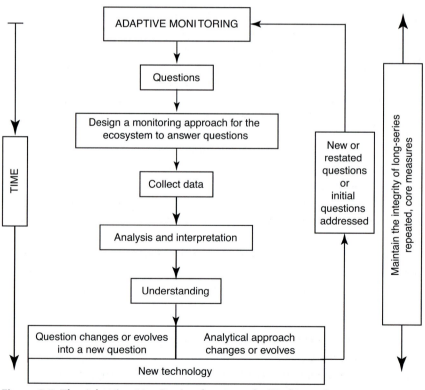

Figure 3.5 The Adaptive Monitoring framework. (Redrawn from Lindenmayer and Likens 2009, with permission from Elsevier)

monitoring can only occur if it is based on questions. Without them, important discoveries cannot be made because discoveries represent answers to questions. This suggestion might seem almost banal but as we shall show in Chapter 4, it is extraordinary how often this initial question-setting step is done poorly or overlooked entirely, even in very large government-funded programs.

Close attention to questions may quickly indicate that long-term research and monitoring are not needed (see Box 1.4 in Chapter 1). Setting clear objectives and framing questions will help resolve squabbles about what to monitor because that will be based on the questions asked. It also will circumvent arguments about whether particular entities are 'indicators'; again because the entities selected for monitoring will be those that are appropriate for answering the questions being posed (see Chapter 2).

A fundamental part of the Adaptive Monitoring paradigm is that the question setting, experimental design, data collection, data analysis, and data interpretation are iterative steps (Figure 3.5). A monitoring program then can evolve and develop in response to new information or new questions. For example, it may be appropriate to alter the frequency of data collection when key entities are changing at rates different than those initially anticipated. An Adaptive Monitoring approach also enables questions to change, new questions to be posed and new protocols to be embraced when, for example, new technology arises to enhance field or laboratory measurements within the overall monitoring framework.

Several authors have highlighted the importance of evolving questions as part of a robust approach to monitoring programs (Hicks and Brydes 1994; Ringold *et al.* 1996). An Adaptive Monitoring approach represents an iterative and linked framework that allows this evolution to take place in a logical way. An important caveat here is that the adoption of new sampling or analytical methods must ensure that the integrity of the long-term data record is neither breached nor distorted. Another caveat is that sometimes particular questions cannot be addressed with a given long-term dataset (that it was not originally designed to address) and an entirely new investigation may need to be established.

In summary, the Adaptive Monitoring framework is scale-independent but new question- and new opportunity-dependent.

A hypothetical example of how the Adaptive Monitoring framework works

The following is a brief example of how adaptive monitoring might work in practice. Preceding and following a management intervention to construct a wastewater treatment plant to lower phosphorus loading to a lake where eutrophication was thought to be driven by excess loading of phosphorus, long-term monitoring of phytoplankton diversity and productivity and water chemistry had been established. This before-after framework had been deliberately set up to guide robust monitoring of the actual impact of this management action on eutrophication of the lake. After a decade of post-construction monitoring, it became apparent that because of changing climate it would also be important to monitor the changes in thermal stratification and duration of ice cover for the lake in addition to water quality, in order to evaluate more precisely the rate of recovery from eutrophication. To adapt the original monitoring scheme to include climate change effects, several issues would need to be resolved. For example: (1) How do these new parameters fit into the conceptual model for eutrophication of this lake? (2) What new question(s) should be posed and new measurements made to address the climate change problem? For example, a possible new question might be: 'Is there an effect of increasing temperature on water circulation patterns and algal productivity in the lake'? (3) What statistically based experimental design would be needed to answer this question? And, (4) How can the integrity of the overall monitoring program be maintained given that new questions have been posed and new or additional monitoring protocols would be required possibly at different times of the year?

Adaptive Monitoring is a general and not a prescriptive framework

The core principles of the Adaptive Monitoring framework with its focus on questions, a conceptual model and an experimental design mean that the approach is relevant to a wide range of circumstances and to all kinds of monitoring, from very simple to very complex programs as well as from mandated monitoring programs usually conducted at a coarse scale to site- or landscape-level curiosity-driven monitoring programs (as defined at the beginning of Chapter 1). However, as illustrated in our hypothetical example above, the Adaptive Monitoring paradigm does not lead to a set of highly specific prescriptions that can be applied uncritically to any given monitoring program. Rather, its specific application will be context-dependent, and will vary in response to the particular problem to be resolved, the questions being posed, and the composition and ecological processes of particular ecosystems. Our approach also emphasises that Adaptive Monitoring is not mindless data collection, but instead pivots on the legitimate scientific practice of posing rigorous questions and carefully designing and implementing appropriate studies to answer them.

The proposed new paradigm of Adaptive Monitoring shares many common elements with the Adaptive Management paradigm (*sensu* Walters 1986), which is much discussed but rarely implemented (Stankey *et al.* 2003; Lindenmayer *et al.* 2007). That is, (**1**) the question-setting step will often be best motivated and implemented by testing management interventions which are relevant to policy options for the management of ecosystems and natural resources (Walters and Holling 1990; Nichols and Williams 2006). (**2**) There is an explicit acknowledgment of ignorance. That is, there are things that are not known that the monitoring work specifically sets out to address (Walters 1986; Williams and Johnson 1995). (**3**) The questions developed for testing are based on *a priori* predictions from a conceptual model suggesting how an ecosystem might function and what the response of monitored entities might be to competing management interventions in that ecosystem, and (**4**) there are strong links between the iterative steps in the Adaptive Monitoring framework which connect question setting with management actions (e.g. an intervention) and an improved understanding of ecosystem or population responses.

Increased future role for Adaptive Monitoring

We hope that the Adaptive Monitoring framework will become increasingly important in the future to help make long-term ecological research and monitoring programs more effective. Novel opportunities for adaptive monitoring will arise because of largely anthropogenic perturbations such as climate change, acid rain, elevated levels of ozone and increased occurrences of large-scale, natural disturbances. These human-accelerated environmental changes represent novel, but unreplicated, 'experimental' opportunities for long-term monitoring. Because such environmental problems are now at the forefront of society's concerns, Adaptive Monitoring will be important in finding solutions to them or designing ways to mitigate their effects. For example, the application of the Adaptive Monitoring framework should help the development of new questions within existing long-term monitoring programs about rapid climate change effects.

In addition, planned experimental manipulation of environmental parameters, particularly at the catchment scale, also will provide vital information for the development of scientific understanding and protocols for managing of natural resources. The scientific value of these manipulated disturbances is evident from the results of long-term monitoring at places like the Hubbard Brook Experimental Forest (see Box 3.5).

BOX 3.5 LONG-TERM RESEARCH AND MONITORING IN THE HUBBARD BROOK EXPERIMENTAL FOREST

The long-term monitoring of hydrologic and chemical fluxes to and from the various watershed-ecosystems of the Hubbard Brook Valley of New Hampshire (air, land and water interactions) is an instructive example of Adaptive Monitoring. Adaptation of the monitoring protocols was necessary because many new questions emerged as a result of the long-term research and monitoring (e.g. see Lawrence and Driscoll 1990; Bailey *et al.* 2003; Likens 2004; Likens *et al.* 2004; Bernhardt *et al.* 2005; Holmes 2007; Likens and Buso 2010a). Over time, long-term monitoring was refined to address each new question better, but without altering the fundamental data-collection format.

These long-term studies have revealed new understanding about several major environmental problems such as acid rain (e.g. Likens *et al.* 1972; Cogbill and Likens 1974; Likens and Bormann 1974; Likens *et al.* 1996; Driscoll *et al.* 2001; Likens 2004); hydrological and biogeochemical response to clearcutting of forests (e.g. Likens *et al.* 1970; Bormann and Likens 1979; Likens *et al.* 1998; Likens *et al.* 2002); salt contamination of surface waters (e.g. Bormann and Likens 1985; Rosenberry *et al.* 1999; Kaushal *et al.* 2005; Likens and Buso 2010b), and long-term legacies of forest disturbance (e.g. Bernhardt *et al.* 2002; Bernhardt *et al.* 2005; Likens and Buso 2009), and have been fundamentally important in the generation of new approaches to management and policy (e.g. Likens *et al.* 1978; Driscoll *et al.* 2001; Likens 2004).

Change is a predominant feature of all ecosystems and has been the impetus of long-term studies of watershed-ecosystems and associated aquatic ecosystems within the Hubbard Brook Valley (Bormann and Likens 1979; Likens and Buso 2009). The characteristics of change in the Hubbard Brook Valley include those brought about by natural biological succession of forest and aquatic ecosystems (e.g. development of soil profiles and organic debris dams) and those caused by disturbance such as acid rain, ice- and wind-storm damage and climate change. Some of the major changes during the past four decades include decreases in concentration and flux of sulphate in precipitation, stream and lake water (Likens *et al.* 2002; Winter and Likens 2009) related to decreases in sulphur dioxide emissions for the source area of the Hubbard Brook Experimental Forest (Butler *et al.* 2001; Likens *et al.* 2001; Butler *et al.* 2003; Likens *et al.* 2005); decreases in concentration and flux of calcium and magnesium and increases in pH of precipitation and stream water (Likens *et al.* 1996; Likens *et al.* 1998; Likens 2004; Likens *et al.* 2005); decreases in maximum snow depth and water content of the snow, while mean annual air temperature, particularly during winter, has increased (Campbell *et al.* 2007); and decreases in bird (Holmes 2007) and salamander populations.

> Long-term records have been indispensable for identifying, documenting and characterising important changes affecting the Hubbard Brook Experimental Forest. As a result of these long-term data, trends have become clearer and more meaningful to managers and policy-makers. Nevertheless, after 46 years of continuous research and monitoring, there continues to be many exciting and compelling questions to pursue with Adaptive Monitoring.

SUMMARY

We have outlined here some of the key features that should characterise effective monitoring programs. They should (1) address well-defined and tractable questions specified prior to the commencement of a monitoring program; (2) be underpinned by rigorous statistical design, and (3) be driven by a human need to know about an ecosystem (e.g. the effects of a pollutant or changes in climate) so that they 'pass the test of management relevance' (*sensu* Russell-Smith *et al.* 2003). Effective monitoring programs will often have other typically interrelated features and we have summarised them in a checklist in Box 3.6.

There are many examples of how long-term data can change perspectives or understanding about how the world works, including 'surprises' or unexpected responses to stresses or disturbances (Chapter 1). Long-term monitoring can invalidate or change preconceived ideas about how ecosystems change with time, by showing how different time steps of observation or analysis (weekly, monthly, annual or decadal) can give different results. An excellent example of the latter is provided in the 'Keeling Curve Lessons' (http://scrippsco2.ucsd.edu) (see Box 3.4).

The Adaptive Monitoring paradigm we have outlined in this chapter is characterised by many of the features in Box 3.6. We believe that Adaptive Monitoring has the potential to improve significantly the record of high-quality, long-term ecological research and monitoring programs worldwide. The Adaptive Monitoring paradigm should increase the credibility of monitoring programs within the scientific community by demonstrating the pivotal roles of the traditional scientific method of posing and then answering questions. It should elicit greater engagement of resource managers by ensuring that the questions posed pass the test of management relevance. It also should encourage and provide confidence to policy-makers and funders in their attempts to be responsible in the use of public funds. Finally, the Adaptive Monitoring paradigm should assist scientists and resource managers in moving beyond protracted debates about how to monitor and what to monitor – debates that have greatly impeded progress in ecological research over the past few decades.

BOX 3.6 SOME CRITICAL COMPONENTS FOR MAINTAINING EFFECTIVE MONITORING PROGRAMS (MODIFIED FROM LIKENS 2007)

- Plots and study sites marked and identified permanently. Detailed descriptions of study areas and field protocols filed in more than one location. Sufficient detail provided so that other investigators can find sites, reproduce calculations and methods at some later date.
- Appropriate and adequate references and/or control sites established at the beginning of the study.
- Availability of appropriate field equipment.
- Long-term security of research sites and field equipment.
- Reliable access to field sites, including availability of safe and reliable vehicles, such as trucks, boats, snowmobiles.
- Careful attention to field and laboratory protocols. Methods and procedures standardised to the extent possible, and inter-calibrated with other organisations or individuals doing similar studies. Calibration of analytical results by comparison against standardised samples. Analytical methods or collection procedures should not be changed without testing fully the effect of the new procedure on the long-term record.
- Frequency for sampling in a time series determined from questions addressed and from analyses of results. Duration of measurements at least as long as the phenomenon being evaluated, or scaled to the frequency of the event or the life history of the organism being studied.
- Methods or procedures developed for one location or study should not be adopted for another area or study without careful testing and justification.
- Strict database management and data storage, including the agility to change with changes in technology. Dataset storage in at least two separate locations to avoid accidental loss. Long-term storage of samples is highly desired.
- 'Fire in the belly' of the project's leadership (a champion for the project).
- Stability and competence of staff.
- Resolution of intellectual property issues at the outset of a project.
- Matching of the scale of monitoring to the spatial and temporal dimensions of the question being addressed.
- Significant time in the field by senior *and* junior scientists working *together.*
- Continuous data sets that are constantly updated, scrutinised for errors and rigorously reviewed.
- Actual *use* of long-term data sets to answer questions.

- Maintenance of a stream of publications to develop project credibility, credentials and outreach.
- Maintenance of scientific independence and integrity of the project by avoiding vested interests.
- Partnerships among scientists, policy-makers and staff from resource management agencies to ensure that long-term work passes the test of management relevance.
- Availability of adequate, sustained and reliable funding.
- Ongoing development and evolution of questions that can use the information from the monitoring program as a framework or operate parallel to it.

REFERENCES

Alewell C, Mitchell MJ, Likens GE and Krouse HR (1999) Sources of stream sulfate at the Hubbard Brook Experimental Forest: long-term analyses using stable isotopes. *Biogeochemistry* **41**, 281–299.

Bailey AS, Hornbeck JW, Campbell JL and Eagar C (2003) Hydrometeorological database for Hubbard Brook Experimental Forest: 1955–2000. Gen. Tech. Report NE-305. USDA Forest Service, Northeastern Research Station, Newtown Square, Pennsylvania.

Bernhardt ES, Hall Jr. RO and Likens GE (2002) Whole-system estimates of nitrification and nitrate uptake in streams of the Hubbard Brook Experimental Forest. *Ecosystems* **5**, 419–430.

Bernhardt ES, Likens GE, Hall Jr. RO, Buso DC, Fisher SG, Burton TM, Meyer JL, McDowell WH, Mayer MS, Bowden WB, Findlay SE, Macneale KH, Stelzer RS and Lowe WH (2005) Can't see the forest for the stream? In-stream processing and terrestrial nitrogen exports. *BioScience* **55**, 219–230.

Bormann FH and Likens GE (1967) Nutrient cycling. *Science* **155**, 424–429.

Bormann FH and Likens GE (1979) *Pattern and Process in a Forested Ecosystem.* Springer-Verlag, New York.

Bormann FH and Likens GE (1985) Air and watershed management and the aquatic ecosystem. In *An Ecosystem Approach to Aquatic Ecology: Mirror Lake and its Environment.* (Ed. GE Likens) pp. 436–444. Springer-Verlag, New York.

Bradstock RA, Williams JE and Gill AM (Eds) (2002) *Flammable Australia: The Fire Regimes and Biodiversity of a Continent.* Cambridge University Press, Melbourne.

Brawn JRD, Robinson SK and Thompson FR (2001) The role of disturbance in the ecology and conservation of birds. *Annual Review of Ecology and Systematics* **32**, 251–276.

Buso DC, Likens GE and Eaton JS (2000) Chemistry of precipitation, stream water and lake water from the Hubbard Brook Ecosystem Study: A record of sampling protocols and analytical procedures. General Tech. Report NE-275. USDA Forest Service, Northeastern Research Station, Newtown Square, Pennsylvania.

Butler TJ, Likens GE and Stunder BJB (2001) Regional-scale impacts of Phase I of the Clean Air Act Amendments in the USA: the relation between emissions and concentrations, both wet and dry. *Atmospheric Environment* **35**, 1015–1028.

Butler TJ, Likens GE, Vermeylen FM and Stunder BJB (2003) The relation between NOx emissions and precipitation NO3- in the eastern USA. *Atmospheric Environment* **37**, 2093–2104.

Campbell JL, Driscoll CT, Eagar C, Likens GE, Siccama TG, Johnson CE, Fahey TJ, Hamburg SP, Holmes RT, Bailey AS and Buso DC (2007) Long-term trends from ecosystem research at the Hubbard Brook Experimental Forest. Gen.Tech. Rep. NRS-17. USDA Forest Service, Northern Research Station, Newtown Square, Pennsylvania.

Carpenter SR (1998) The need for long-scale experiments to assess and predict the response of ecosystems to perturbation. In *Successes, Limitations, and Frontiers in Ecosystem Science.* (Eds ML Pace and PM Groffman) pp. 287–312. Springer-Verlag, New York.

Charles DF (Ed) (1991) *Acidic Deposition and Aquatic Ecosystems: Regional case Studies.* Springer-Verlag, New York.

Clark TW (2002) *The Policy Process. A Practical Guide for Natural Resource Professionals.* Yale University Press, New Haven, Connecticut.

Cogbill CV and Likens GE (1974) Acid precipitation in the northeastern United States. *Water Resources Research* **10**, 1133–1137.

Danell K, Bergström R, Duncan P and Pastor J (Eds) (2006) *Large Mammalian Herbivores, Ecosystem Dynamics, and Conservation.* Cambridge University Press, UK.

De Jager N and Pastor J (2009) Declines in moose population density on Isle Royale and accompanying changes in landscape patterns. *Landscape Ecology*, in press.

DeJager N, Pastor J and Hodgson A (2009) The effects of moose browsing on plant geometry regulates subsequent food intake rates across the landscape. *Ecological Monographs*, in press.

Driscoll CT, Lawrence GB, Bulger AJ, Butler TJ, Cronan CS, Eagar C, Fallon Lambert K, Likens GE, Stoddard JL and Weathers KC (2001) Acidic deposition in the northeastern United States: sources and inputs, ecosystem effects, and management strategies. *BioScience* **51**, 180–198.

Edwards A, Kennett R, Price O, Russell-Smith J, Spiers G and Woinarski J (2003) Monitoring the impacts of fire regimes on vegetation in northern Australia: an example from Kakadu National Park. *International Journal of Wildland Fire* **12**, 427–440.

Field SA, O'Connor PJ, Tyre AJ and Possingham HP (2007) Making monitoring meaningful. *Austral Ecology* **32**, 485–491.

Franklin JF, Harmon ME and Swanson FJ (1999) Complementary roles of research and monitoring: lessons from the U.S. LTER Program and Tierra del Fuego. Paper presented to the Symposium. Paper presented at 'Toward a unified framework for inventorying and monitoring forest ecosystem resources', Guadalajara, Mexico, November 1998.

Gibbons P, Zammit C, Youngentob K, Possingham HP, Lindenmayer DB, Bekessy S, Burgman M, Colyvan M, Considine M, Felton A, Hobbs R, Hurley C, McAlpine C, McCarthy MA, Moore J, Robinson D, Salt D and Wintle B (2008) Some practical suggestions for improving engagement between policy makers and researchers in natural resource management. *Ecological Restoration and Management* **9**, 182–186.

Grove SJ (2007) Ecological research coverage at the Warra LTER Site, Tasmania: a gap analysis based on a conceptual ecological model. *Tasforests* **15**, 43–53.

Hicks BB and Bryde, TG (1994) A strategy for integrated monitoring. *Environmental Management* **18**, 1–12.

Hirsch RM, Hamilton PA and Miller TL (2006) U.S. Geological Survey perspective on water-quality monitoring and assessment. *Journal of Environmental Monitoring* **8**, 512–518.

Holmes RT (2007) Understanding population change in migratory songbirds: long-term and experimental studies of Neotropical migrants in breeding and wintering areas. *Ibis* **S2:149**, 2–13.

Hong L and Page SE (2004) Groups of diverse problem solvers can outperform groups of high-ability problem solvers. *Proceedings of the National Academy of Sciences* **101**, 16385–16389.

Kaushal SS, Groffman PM, Likens GE, Belt KT, Stack WP, Kelly VR, Band LE and Fisher GT (2005) Increased salinization of fresh water in the northeastern United States. *Proceedings of the National Academy of Sciences* **102**, 13517–13520.

Keeling CD, Chin JF and Whorf TP (1996) Increased activity of northern vegetation inferred from atmospheric CO2 measurements. *Nature* **382**, 146–149.

Keeling CD, Whorf TP, Wahlen M and van der Plicht J (1995) Interannual extremes in the rate of rise of atmospheric carbon dioxide since 1980. *Nature* **357**, 666–670.

King L (2004) Impacting policy through science and education. *Preventative Veterinary Medicine* **62**, 185–192.

Krebs CJ (1991) The experimental paradigm and long-term population studies. *Ibis* **133**, 2–8.

Krebs CJ, Carrier P, Boutin S, Boonstra R and Hofer EJ (2008) Mushroom crops in relation to weather in the southwestern Yukon. *Botany* **86**, 1497–1502.

Landres PB, Verner J and Thomas JW (1988) Ecological uses of vertebrate indicator species: a critique. *Conservation Biology* **2**, 316–328.

Laurance W and Luizao R (2007) Driving a wedge into the Amazon. *Nature* **448**, 409–410.

Lawrence GB and Driscoll CT (1990) Longitudinal patterns of concentration-discharge relationships in streamwater draining the Hubbard Brook Experimental Forest, New Hampshire. *Journal of Hydrology* **116**, 147–165.

Likens GE (Ed.) (1989) *Long-term Studies in Ecology: Approaches and Alternatives.* Springer-Verlag, New York.

Likens GE (1992) *The Ecosystem Approach: Its Use and Abuse. Excellence in Ecology, Volume 3.* Ecology Institute, Oldendorf/Luhe, Germany.

Likens GE (2004) Some perspectives on long-term biogeochemical research from the Hubbard Brook Ecosystem Study. *Ecology* **85**, 2355–2362.

Likens,GE and Bormann, FH (1974) Acid rain: a serious regional environmental problem. *Science* **184**, 1176–1179.

Likens GE, Bormann, FH and Johnson, NM (1972) Acid rain. *Environment* **14**, 33–40.

Likens GE, Bormann FH, Johnson NM, Fisher DW and Pierce RS (1970) Effects of forest cutting and herbicide treatment on nutrient budgets in the Hubbard Brook watershed-ecosystem. *Ecological Monographs* **40**, 23–47.

Likens GE, Bormann FH, Pierce RS and Reiners WA (1978) Recovery of a deforested ecosystem. *Science* **199**, 492–496.

Likens GE and Buso DC (2010a) Long-term changes in streamwater chemistry following disturbance in the Hubbard Brook Experimental Forest, USA. *Verhandlungen der Internationalen Vereinigung für Theoretische und Angewandte Limnologie* **30**, (In press).

Likens GE and Buso DC (2010b) Salinization of Mirror Lake by road salt. *Water, Air and Soil Pollution* **205**, 205–214.

Likens GE, Buso DC and Butler TJ (2005) Long-term relationships between SO2 and NOX emissions and SO42- and NO3- concentration in bulk deposition at the Hubbard Brook Experimental Forest, New Hampshire. *Journal of Environmental Monitoring* **7**, 964–968.

Likens GE, Butler TJ and Buso DC (2001) Long- and short-term changes in sulfate deposition: effects of the 1990 Clean Air Act amendments. *Biogeochemistry* **52**, 1–11.

Likens GE, Dresser BK and Buso DC (2004) Short-term, temperature response in forest floor and soil to ice storm disturbance in a northern hardwood forest. *Northern Journal of Applied Forestry* **21**, 209–219.

Likens GE, Driscoll CT and Buso DC (1996) Long-term effects of acid rain: response and recovery of a forest ecosystem. *Science* **272**, 244–246.

Likens GE, Driscoll CT, Buso DC, Mitchell MJ, Lovett GM, Bailey SW, Siccama TG, Reiners WA and Alewell C (2002) The biogeochemistry of sulfur at Hubbard Brook. *Biogeochemistry* **60**, 235–316.

Likens GE, Driscoll CT, Buso DC, Siccama TG, Johnson CE, Lovett GM, Fahey TJ, Reiners WA, Ryan DF, Martin CW and Bailey SW (1998) The biogeochemistry of calcium at Hubbard Brook. *Biogeochemistry* **41**, 89–173.

Likens GE and Franklin JF (2009) Ecosystem thinking in the Northern Forest – and beyond. *BioScience* **59**, 511–513.

Likens GE, Wright RF, Galloway JN and Butler TJ (1979) Acid rain. *Scientific American* **24**, 43–51.

Lindenmayer DB, Craig SA, Linga T and Tanton MT (1991) Public participation in stagwatching surveys for a rare mammal – applications for environmental education. *Australian Journal of Environmental Education* **7**, 63–70.

Lindenmayer DB and Cunningham RB (1997) Patterns of co-occurrence among arboreal marsupials in the forests of central Victoria, southeastern Australia. *Australian Journal of Ecology* **22**, 340–346.

Lindenmayer DB, Cunningham RB, MacGregor C and Incoll RD (2003) A long-term monitoring study of the population dynamics of arboreal marsupials in the Central Highlands of Victoria. *Biological Conservation* **110**, 161–167.

Lindenmayer DB and Franklin JF (2002) *Conserving Forest Biodiversity: A Comprehensive Multiscaled Approach*. Island Press, Washington.

Lindenmayer DB, Hobbs R, Montague-Drake R, Alexandra J, Bennett A, Burgman M, Cale P, Calhoun A, Cramer V, Cullen P, Driscoll D, Fahrig L, Fischer J, Franklin J, Haila Y, Hunter M, Gibbons P, Lake S, Luck G, McIntyre S, Mac Nally R, Manning A, Miller J, Mooney H, Noss R, Possingham H, Saunders D, Schmiegelow F, Scott M, Simberloff D, Sisk T, Walker B, Wiens J, Woinarski J and Zavaleta E (2007) A checklist for ecological management of landscapes for conservation. *Ecology Letters* **10**, 1–14.

Lindenmayer DB and Likens GE (2009) Adaptive monitoring - a new paradigm for long-term research and monitoring. *Trends in Ecology and Evolution* **24**, 482–486.

Lindenmayer DB, MacGregor C, Wood JT, Cunningham RB, Crane M, Michael D, Montague-Drake R and Brown D (2008) Testing hypotheses associated with bird recovery after wildfire. *Ecological Applications* **18**, 1967–1983.

Lindenmayer DB, Margules CR and Botkin DB (2000) Indicators of biodiversity for ecologically sustainable forest management. *Conservation Biology* **14**, 941–950.

Lovett GM, Burns DA, Driscoll CT, Jemkins JC, Mitchell MJ, Rustad L, Shanley JB, Likens GE and Haeuber R (2007) Who needs environmental monitoring? *Frontiers in Ecology and the Environment* **5**, 253–260.

Loyn RH (1985) Bird populations in successional forests of Mountain Ash *Eucalyptus regnans* in Central Victoria. *Emu* **85**, 213–230.

Ludwig D, Mangel M and Haddad B (2001) Ecology, conservation and public policy. *Annual Review of Ecology and Systematics* **32**, 481–517.

Martin J, Kitchens WM and Hines JE (2007) Importance of well-designed monitoring programs for the conservation of endangered species: case study of the Snail Kite. *Conservation Biology* **21**, 472–481.

McInnes PF, Naiman RJ, Pastor J and Cohen Y (1992) Effects of moose browsing on vegetation and litterfall of the boreal forest, Isle Royale, Michigan, USA. *Ecology* **73**, 2059–2075.

Nichols JD and Williams BK (2006) Monitoring for conservation. *Trends in Ecology and Evolution* **21**, 668–673.

Norton DA (1996) Monitoring biodiversity in New Zealand's terrestrial ecosystems. In *Papers from a seminar series on biodiversity.* (Eds B McFadgen and S Simpson) pp. 19–41. Department of Conservation, Wellington, New Zealand.

Pastor J, Dewey B, Moen R, White M, Mladenoff D and Cohen Y (1998) Spatial patterns in the moose-forest-soil ecosystem on Isle Royale, Michigan, USA. *Ecological Applications* **8**, 411–424.

Pastor J, Dewey B, Naiman RJ, McInnes PF and Cohen Y (1993) Moose browsing and soil fertility in the boreal forests of Isle Royale National Park. *Ecology* **74**, 467–480.

Pastor J, Naiman RJ, Dewey B and McInnes P (1988) Moose, microbes, and the boreal forest. *BioScience* **38**, 770–777.

Persson I-L, Nilsson MB, Pastor J, Eriksson T, Bergström R and Danell K (2009) Depression of belowground respiration rates at simulated high moose population densities in boreal forests. *Ecology*, (In press).

Persson I-L, Pastor J, Danell K and Bergström R (2005) Impact of moose population density and forest productivity on the production and composition of litter in boreal forests. *Oikos* **108**, 297–306.

Peters RH (1991) *A Critique for Ecology.* Cambridge University Press, Cambridge.

Pielke RA (2007) *The Honest Broker: Making Sense of Science in Policy and Politics.* Cambridge University Press, Cambridge, England.

Ringold PL, Alegria J, Czaplwski RL, Mulder BS, Tolle T and Burnett K (1996) Adaptive monitoring design for ecosystem management. *Ecological Applications* **6**, 745–747.

Rosenberry DO, Bukaveckas PA, Buso DC, Likens GE, Shapiro AM and Winter TC (1999) Movement of road salt to a small New Hampshire lake. *Water, Air, and Soil Pollution* **109**, 179–206.

Russell-Smith J, Whitehead PJ, Cook GD and Hoare JL (2003) Response of *Eucalyptus*-dominated savanna to frequent fires: lessons from Munmarlary 1973–1996. *Ecological Monographs* **73**, 349–375.

Sauer JR, Pendleton GW and Peterjohn BG (1998) Evaluating causes of population change in North American insectivorous songbirds. *Conservation Biology* **10**, 465–478.

Schindler DW, Mills KH, Malley DF, Findlay DL, Shearer JA, Davies IJ, Turner MA, Linsey GA and Cruikshank DR (1985) Long-term ecosystem stress: the effects of years of experimental acidification on a small lake. *Science* **228**, 1395–1401.

Smith AP, Lindenmayer D, Begg RJ, Macfarlane MA, Seebeck JH and Suckling GC (1989) Evaluation of the stag-watching technique for census of possums and gliders in tall open forest. *Australian Wildlife Research* **16**, 575–580.

Spellerberg IF (1994) *Monitoring Ecological Change.* Second edition. Cambridge University Press, Cambridge, UK.

Stankey GH, Bormann BT, Ryan C, Shindler B, Sturtevant V, Clark RN and Philpot C (2003) Adaptive management and the Northwest Forest Plan – rhetoric and reality. *Journal of Forestry* **101**, 40–46.

Stokstad E (2008) Canada's Experimental Lakes. *Science* **322**, 1316–1319.

Strayer DL, Glitzenstein JS, Jones C, Kolasa J, Likens GE, McDonnell M, Parker GG and Pickett STA (1986) Long-term ecological studies: an illustrated account of their design, operation, and importance to ecology. Institute of Ecosystem Studies, Millbrook, New York.

Taylor BL and Gerrodette T (1993) The uses of statistical power in conservation biology: the Vaquita and Northern Spotted Owl. *Conservation Biology* **7**, 489–500.

Thomas L and Martin K (1996) The importance of analysis method for Breeding Bird Survey population trend estimates. *Conservation Biology* **10**, 479–490.

Walters C (1997) Adaptive policy design: thinking at large spatial scales. In *Wildlife and Landscape Ecology.* (Ed. J Bissonette) pp. 386–394. Springer-Verlag, New York.

Walters CJ (1986) Adaptive management of renewable resources. Macmillan, New York.

Walters CJ and Holling CS (1990) Large scale management experiments and learning by doing. *Ecology* **71**, 2060–2068.

Weathers KC, Strayer DL and Likens GE (Eds) (2009) *Fundamentals of Ecosystem Science.* Elsevier Academic Press, New York.

Welsh AH, Cunningham RB and Chambers RL (2000) Methodology for estimating the abundance of rare animals: seabird nesting on North East Herald Cay. *Biometrics* **56**, 22–30.

Whelan RJ (1995) *The Ecology of Fire.* Cambridge University Press, Cambridge.

Williams BK and Johnson FA (1995) Adaptive management and the regulation of waterfowl harvests. *Wildlife Society Bulletin* **23**, 430–436.

Winter TC and Likens GE (Eds) (2009) *Mirror Lake: Interactions among Air, Land and Water.* University of California Press, Los Angeles.

Woodward A, Jenkins K and Schreiner EG (1999) The role of ecological theory in long-term monitoring: Report on a workshop. *Natural Areas Journal* **19**, 223–233.

Yoccoz NG, Nichols JD and Boulinier T (2001) Monitoring of biological diversity in space and time. *Trends in Ecology and Evolution* **16**, 446–453.

Chapter 4

The problematic, the effective and the ugly – some case studies

The previous two chapters outlined some of the characteristics of what we considered to be poor or failed monitoring programs (Chapter 2) and good and effective monitoring programs (Chapter 3), respectively. In this chapter, we reinforce some of these points through a series of case studies. The case studies cover terrestrial, marine, and inland aquatic landscapes; they come from a range of places (three continents); they represent both mandated monitoring and monitoring programs driven by investigator curiosity. They include environmental monitoring (e.g. nutrients and water flows) as well as monitoring of populations of particular organisms. In each case study, we briefly describe the location of the work, the broad aims of the study, some of its important negative and positive features, and an occasional anecdote. We also give a web address for each case study so that readers can obtain further information. These case studies were selected from a large number that could have been highlighted, but these were chosen to illustrate the range of features we deemed important within the scope of this small book.

We wrote this chapter with great trepidation because we realise that we will almost certainly deeply offend many people, including many friends and colleagues who are truly outstanding scientists. It would therefore have been far easier to leave this chapter out of the book entirely! However, we felt it was absolutely necessary to write this chapter for three primary reasons. First, we wish to illustrate with clear and tangible examples what features we believe underpin good long-term research and monitoring programs and those that are problematic or that fail. Second, we wanted to highlight some aspects of studies for which we ourselves have been personally responsible by showing that they are far from perfect. The third reason we felt compelled to write this chapter was to demonstrate ways that long-term monitoring programs could be improved. We passionately believe this goal is critical if the scientific and management communities are to address the mind-boggling number of major environmental problems facing humanity. In fact, this goal underlies the reason we wrote this book.

We readily acknowledge that our assessments of the case studies arise from our value judgements, but then this book is based on our personal perspectives. We have attempted to make our criticisms carefully because

---

BOX 4.1 TREPIDATION

Writing this chapter was nerve-racking and certainly far from 'career-enhanc-ing' as we have been critical of a major province-level program (in Alberta, Canada) and a number of national-level programs (the NEON and EMAP initia-tives in the USA, and TERN in Australia). We had concerns for several reasons. First, these efforts were characterised at the outset by either a lack of focused questions or only very general questions that may not readily be tractable from a scientific perspective. Second, in the case of NEON and TERN, they are eco-logical and environmental infrastructure initiatives with questions 'retro-fitted' after the infrastructure had been decided upon, leading to a risk that the wrong infrastructure may be targeted for investment. Third, they appeared to lack a conceptual model directly related to ecosystem function, a robust underpin-ning experimental design, or both.

Each of these programs may, in fact, prove to be successful and exciting new discoveries may well emerge from them. Indeed, we sincerely hope that this is the case. NEON has not officially begun and TERN only barely so as we write this book. However, we do believe that the lack of the key ingredi-ents of successful monitoring programs – motivating questions, a conceptual model, and a robust experimental design – means that these very large pro-grams have considerable risks of mistakes being made and large sums of money being used inefficiently and ineffectively. These deficiencies may not make ecologists look good in the eyes of the public and could endanger future funding for monitoring. Few long-term monitoring programs or funding initiatives can afford such inefficiencies. This is a basis for our concerns and we argue that key characteristics such as well-developed questions and appropriate experimental design are fundamental to the effectiveness and success of monitoring programs.

we know that the proponents of these activities are likely to be very well intentioned. Our definition of an effective or problematic case study was that it was not particularly relevant on a cost-benefit analysis to management, provided inadequate or incorrect answers to key resource management problems, or was not scientifically productive. We argue that these problems mean the work breaches many of the principles that we outline as being important in the Adaptive Monitoring framework. We note, however, that all the case studies of ineffective monitoring have some good points and we believe there are important opportunities to improve them. Indeed, if the commentary we have provided on any of the case studies were to lead to improvements in any of the monitoring programs we have outlined, then we would feel that such an outcome was an important achievement.

THE PROBLEMATIC

PPBio Australasia

Web address: www.griffith.edu.au/ppbio, http://ppbio.inpa.gov.br

The Program for Planned Biodiversity and Ecosystem Research (PPBio) Australasia is a standardised research and monitoring platform designed to promote the collection, storing and sharing of biological information (Hero *et al.* 2009). The documentation accompanying the PPBio sites in south-eastern Queensland suggests that an array of measurements can be made using this standardised platform, including vegetation composition and biomass, soils, hydrology, amphibians, birds, vegetation structure, lizards, leaf litter, mammals, spiders and invertebrates. It was suggested that vascular plants, birds, and beetles would be 'indicator taxa' of value for monitoring.

The PPBio approach has been implemented in Brazil (Magnusson *et al.* 2005) and then adapted for use in eastern Australia (Hero *et al.* 2009). There is also an extension to Chitwan National Park in Nepal (Hero *et al.* 2009). The PPBio method is based on a 5-km × 5-km grid of survey trails within which is located a grid of 30 permanently marked 1-ha plots. In Australia, this approach has been implemented in two areas in south-eastern Queensland, one within the Karawatha Forest Park in the city of Brisbane comprising 33 plots spaced at 500-m intervals, and another at Lake Broadwater with 19 plots set out at 1-km intervals (Hero *et al.* 2009). A wide range of attributes are measured at each plot. Funding for the PPBio program in south-eastern Queensland comes from several sources including the Brisbane City Council, South East Queensland Catchments Inc. and Griffith University (Hero *et al.* 2009).

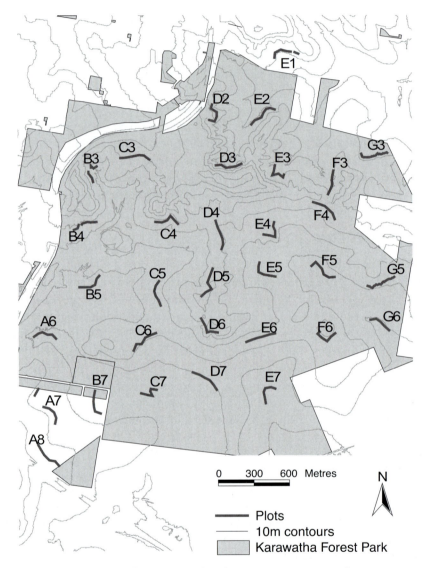

Figure 4.1 The layout of a PPBio grid with survey points spaced at a set interval of 1-km grid squares. (Redrawn from Hero *et al.* 2009)

One of the stated aims of PPBio is to establish PPBio grids in all the major ecoregions of Australia, make these areas akin to Long-term Ecological Research sites (LTERs) such as those established in the USA, allowing for '*comparable assessment of biodiversity indicators across a range of spatio-temporal scales*' (Hero *et al.* 2009). Such assessments include moni-toring of the effects of climate change on biodiversity.

We believe that the aims of the PPBio approach are noble ones and the champions of the method are very well intentioned and enthusiastic. How-ever, we also have concerns that the approach suffers from some of the deficiencies we outline below for the Alberta Biodiversity Monitoring Pro-gram (ABMP).

Paucity of questions

From our reading of documents available to us, the PPBio approach does not appear to be guided by well-defined and testable questions about eco-system function or the dynamics of populations. The design of the work is not characterised by key contrasts in environmental conditions which would allow inferences to be made about the effects of an intervention in one place versus no intervention in another.

Lack of conceptual model

PPBio appears to lack a conceptual model that lays out how a targeted eco-system might function or how it might respond to intervention. Data gath-ered from the approach may therefore not assist in resolving the reasons or mechanisms for any changes that might occur in biodiversity or ecosystem processes.

One size fits all

The PPBio recommends a highly standardised survey framework for all sites and plots within sites (Figure 4.1). This framework assumes that the same general survey protocol will be appropriate for the array of entities proposed to be measured in PPBio. However, this assumption may be read-ily violated. The spatial scale might be the correct one for small reptiles, but inappropriate for more mobile species that range over larger areas, like birds. A related issue is that a highly standardised protocol assumes that it is appropriate to measure precisely the same list of entities at all places. We have outlined in Chapter 2 why this is problematic and firmly suggested that the entities selected for measurement should be guided by the ques-tions being asked. For example, surveys of reptiles may be useful in a highly reptile-rich region like south-eastern Queensland where responses to fire might be a critical aspect of the environment, but they may be of limited value in other jurisdictions like tropical Amazonia where other ecological features, like forest structure and plant species composition, have a far greater impact on biodiversity and biotic responses.

Statistical design

A lack of questions means that it is difficult to assess the efficacy of the experimental design. However, we believe there may be some potential problems with it. First, the spatial clustering of plots in the standardised grid risks pseudo-replication (Hurlbert 1984) for some groups (e.g. birds). Second, in highly variable ecosystems such as the ones being studied in south-eastern Queensland, a survey comprised of ~30 plots may have limited statistical power to detect trends or effects. Third, there appears to be limited stratification to guide plot selection other than space – the plots are distributed on a 1-km × 1-km grid spacing. Fourth, the design does not appear to comprise strong contrasts to help quantify or interpret the effects of management interventions or the reasons for changes in measured attributes over time.

The PPBio approach is undoubtedly an interesting one and is strongly motivated by frustrations that biodiversity monitoring worldwide has been poor and uncoordinated (Hero *et al.* 2009). Despite what we believe are serious problems resulting from a paucity of questions and the overall survey design, PPBio has some positive aspects including limited bureaucracy, many well-developed partnerships including those with the community, and an enthusiastic and highly dedicated advocate. The approach is also relatively inexpensive (at this stage of its development), particularly in comparison with other similar kinds of one-size-fits-all methods for long-term ecological research and monitoring programs such as ABMP.

The Alberta Biodiversity Monitoring Program (ABMP)

Web address: www.abmi.ca

Alberta is a large, resource-rich province in western Canada. It supports globally significant forestry and energy industries and is home to more than 70 000 species of native vertebrates and invertebrates. The Alberta Biodiversity Monitoring Program (ABMP) aims to track changes in about 2000 of these species or approximately 3% of the vertebrate and invertebrate taxa estimated to live in the province. Changes in biodiversity will be tracked at two spatial scales: at individual field sites and large, spatial scales (presumably at landscape scales) using aerial photography and satellite imagery (Alberta Biodiversity Monitoring Institute 2009a; Alberta Biodiversity Monitoring Program 2009).

Background information for the ABMP indicates that it aims to monitor 1656 sites at points evenly spaced in a 20- × 20-km grid across the entire province (Figure 4.2). The list of entities to be monitored is large as shown in Table 4.1. The plan is to survey the groups and attributes in Table 4.1 at

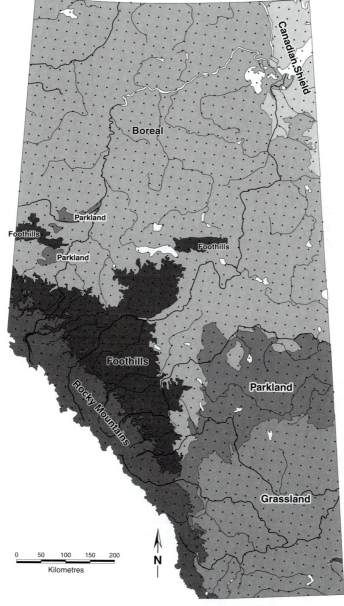

adapted from Alberta Biodiversity Monitoring Institute
by Clive Hilliker, The Australian National University

Figure 4.2 The proposed survey design for the Alberta Biodiversity
Monitoring Institute. (Redrawn from Alberta Biodiversity Monitoring
Institute 2009a; Alberta Biodiversity Monitoring Program 2009)

Table 4.1 Proposed list of target entities for monitoring in the ABMI project. (Drawn from various ABMI documents)

Terrestrial species	Wetland species	Species in lakes and rivers	Terrestrial habitat	Wetland habitat	Landscape habitat	Human footprint
Winter mammals	Mammals	Fish	Physical and ecological characteristics	Wetland size and depth	% composition of habitat types	Urbanisation
Birds	Birds	Benthic algae	Trees, snags, coarse woody debris	Water physio-chemistry	Diversity of habitat types	Agricultural footprint
Vascular plants	Vascular plants	Macro-invertebrates	Habitat structure		Patch size distribution	Forestry footprint
Bryophytes	Invertebrates	Vascular plants				Energy footprint
Lichens		Phytoplankton				Linear features
Fungi		Zooplankton				
Springtails						
Mites						

between 330–375 sites annually and hence visit all 1656 sites every five years (Alberta Biodiversity Monitoring Institute 2009a; Alberta Biodiversity Monitoring Program 2009). The background information available to us for ABMP indicates that the initiative has a well-developed governance structure and will produce five major reports on the state of Alberta's biodiversity over a five-year cycle, with one report published each year. A project as large and ambitious as this is costly and the estimated annual operating cost is just under $CAN10 million.

Some strong claims have been made about the ABMP, such as that it **'is perhaps the most advanced biodiversity monitoring program in the world'** (Alberta Biodiversity Monitoring Program 2009). We remain unsure of these claims because our reading of the documentation available for ABMP leads us to believe ABMP has some problems. We outline some concerns below.

Paucity of questions

The documentation we read for ABMP did not contain information on the questions that were being posed. As we have outlined elsewhere in this book, we believe it is difficult to gauge progress when there are no clearly defined or tractable scientifically based questions being asked to guide a project. In addition, the statistical design of the project (see below) may not be an appropriate one for answering particular questions after the spatial array of monitoring sites had been implemented.

Statistical design

The design of ABMP is an interesting one that is somewhat unusual for a monitoring program. We found it difficult to assess the design critically because we were unable to find clearly defined questions against which to determine its suitability. It appears that the 'stratification' is based on space (Figure 4.2); i.e. the sites are distributed evenly across the province. In some cases the distribution of key organisms and attributes of interest (see Table 4.1) may be strongly influenced by other factors, which seem to us to be perhaps better ones on which to stratify. For example, the age of the forest and level of logging disturbance might be among the factors more likely to influence terrestrial boreal forest taxa. Hence, some direct assessment of trend patterns and logging impacts on those species might be better determined from contrasts between sites before and after they are logged and matched with 'control sites' that remain unlogged. In addition, the spatial design of the sites makes it likely that rare environments will be represented by few replicates. However, these rare environments may well support rare species of conservation and/or management concern for which it may be critically important to assess their status over time (Burton *et al.* 2003). The frequency of surveys (every five to seven years at a given site) also may be an issue as it might not be well matched to quantify some of the key ecological phenomena of interest in the ecosystems of Alberta (e.g. outbreaks of beetles that kill large areas of forest).

Passivity

We feel that ABMP is probably best defined as a passive monitoring program (see Chapter 1); i.e. it is largely aimed at tracking change over time in the province of Alberta. Hence, the project is not characterised by management interventions – which we believe will often be important for the effectiveness of monitoring programs (see Chapter 3), particularly for documenting **why** changes have occurred. In fact, early documentation for ABMP notes that '*the intent of monitoring is not to understand why the change has occurred*' (Shank *et al.* 2002). We believe that this approach may make it difficult to identify the mechanisms underlying the trend patterns that may emerge from the program. It also may curtail predictive ability of any findings and hence possibly limit the potential for proactive environmental management.

Laundry list

The ABMP is a very ambitious initiative and aims to survey a large number of things (Table 4.1). Our concern here is the risk of a large number of things being measured poorly rather than a few things measured well. There is also an assumption that the statistical design and the spatial scale of sites will be appropriate for all of the target groups, ranging from zooplankton to wide-ranging winter mammals. We believe that this assumption may not hold. Moreover, although the governance structure for ABMP is seeking to secure a long-term endowment, which is laudable, the very large number of sites (many of them remote), coupled with the very large number of entities being measured, could eventually be financially untenable and ultimately lead to the collapse of the monitoring program. We note that from examining the ABMP website, between 2003 and 2009 in the Lower Athabasca Region in Alberta (the hotspot for oil sands operations), 68 of the proposed 235 permanent survey sites were visited. Thus, it appears to us that the ABMP may currently lack the human resources to undertake the proposed monitoring protocols for one of the most significant ecological regions in the province of Alberta. Moreover, again based on a report on the ABMP website, 52 bird species (of the ~150 species which occur in the Lower Athabasca Region) and 97 vascular plants (of the ~500 species which occur in the Lower Athabasca Region) have been surveyed at the 68 sites in that time.

Lack of conceptual model

We have argued that a conceptual model of how an ecosystem works is a key part of effective monitoring and a pivotal part of Adaptive Monitoring (see Chapter 3). However, we could find no conceptual model for ABMP (e.g. Farr *et al.* 1999; Alberta Biodiversity Monitoring Program 2005; Alberta Biodiversity Monitoring Program 2009), although this oversight is common to many monitoring programs, including some of our own (see the case study on Victorian forests below). The lack of a conceptual model, coupled with a paucity of *a priori* questions and management interventions (or other kinds of interventions), further suggests to us that ABMP has many of the characteristics of both mandated and passive monitoring programs (see Chapter 1). We therefore reiterate our concern that the status of particular entities will be documented at particular points in time, but there may be limited opportunity to determine why those entities have changed and the ecological mechanism influencing the emergent pattern will not be discovered.

Complex aggregation issues

One of the aims of ABMP is to produce indices that reflect the state of biodiversity in Alberta (Alberta Biodiversity Monitoring Program 2009). For example, an 'intactness' index was created to reflect the status of biodiversity with particular regions in Alberta (Alberta Biodiversity Monitoring Institute 2009b; Lamb *et al.* 2009). These kinds of indices can be useful for generating reports and communicating to politicians and government officials, especially those who want 'one number'. However, such indices need to be constructed very carefully and the assumptions underlying them need to be well understood and clearly articulated (Lamb *et al.* 2009). Indeed, there are vexed issues with creating a composite, scientifically robust index from an amalgam of sub-indices (e.g. see Van Horne and Wiens 1991; Lindenmayer and Burgman 2005) and the results can sometimes be misleading (Wright-Stow and Winterbourn 2003). Moreover, it is sometimes not clear how coarsely scaled summary data can be used to identify trends for biodiversity or how these rather crude trends would be useful to assist on-the-ground resource management, such as in guiding targeted management interventions to solve a particular environmental problem or protect a rare species.

BOX 4.2 REJOINDER: AN ALTERNATIVE SET OF PERSPECTIVES ON ABMP

The ABMP is a different approach to monitoring that is quite unlike any other we have seen to date. We touch on some of these different perspectives and approaches below because in no way do we wish to see our criticisms lead to ABMP being irreparably damaged or possibly even terminated. These outcomes are far from our goals in offering criticisms.

The proponents of ABMP believe that a lack of stratification (other than spatially) is important to: (**1**) provide sufficient sites in any given region to allow suitable regional reporting of trends, and, (**2**) detect shifts in the distributions of species with climate change. In addition, ABMP aims to quantify the cumulative effects of multiple environmental stressors on biodiversity and overall environmental integrity. In particular, the approach seeks to determine how much human modification of landscapes can take place before significant impacts on biota and other measures of environmental integrity become evident. These are interesting perspectives because the province of Alberta is subject to many major forms of environmental perturbation including oil and gas exploration, and widespread industrial logging. Finally, it is believed that the approach taken in the ABMP is appropriate so as not to foreclose future options for monitoring environmental changes that may presently be unforeseen. Despite the novelty of the thinking underpinning ABMP, we nevertheless re-iterate our concerns that the current spatial stratification for ABMP is statistically unusual and may not be the most statistically and ecologically efficient study design. In addition, we are concerned that the current design may not be effective at teasing apart the effects of multiple stressors and determining the underlying causes of any changes that are observed. We therefore believe that an Adaptive Monitoring approach might be best applied to the ABMP.

The essentially passive nature of the ABMP approach was developed because the architects of the program felt that designed monitoring programs can fail the test of management relevance, including being conducted at a scale that is not meaningful for detecting cumulative effects (such as those across entire landscapes). Furthermore, a passive approach was advocated because it was not clear what future problems might arise that need to be monitored. Again, we have concerns that this passive approach to monitoring might not produce the desired results, especially in terms of: (**1**) being able to tease apart the relative effects of different stressors leading to cumulative impacts, (**2**) effectively diagnosing the reasons for the observed changes, and (**3**) being able to effectively respond to currently unforeseen new stressors. We also believe that our adaptive monitoring approach is well suited to changing a monitoring program in response to future problems that may arise but which are presently unknown.

> The extensive suite of entities initially proposed for monitoring (see Table 4.1) has apparently recently been pared down to make the monitoring effort more tractable, especially given the practical realities of surveying numerous remote sites. This reduction is important because of an appreciation for monitoring key parameters well rather than trying to monitor too many things badly (see Chapters 2 and 3). We view this as a very positive step for ABMP.
>
> A considerable amount of thinking and background work has been invested in developing questions for ABMP, but unfortunately this is not reflected in the literature accompanying the initiative. We hope that the proponents of the program might address this deficiency in the near future so that the basis for the monitoring might be made more transparent.

We acknowledge that our assessment of ABMP is somewhat critical and some of it may be unjustified or inappropriate as the project has developed and matured (see Box 4.2). Nevertheless, we do see some very positive aspects to the initiative. First, the proponents of ABMP have clearly given considerable thought to ways of generating sufficient long-term funding to maintain the initiative. Few monitoring programs do that at the beginning. Second, although the governance structure seems large, the approach to bring together many stakeholders and forge partnerships is a valuable one. Third, while the ABMP has the potential to create an extremely valuable set of baseline datasets, we do believe there might be a distinct opportunity for adding carefully selected sites to allow for rigorous quantification of the mechanisms giving rise to key temporal trends in biodiversity.

Our hope is that the perspectives we have set out above might stimulate discussion about many topics such as the questions being posed, the experimental design underpinning ABMP, and the large array of species and attributes being measured. We believe that lively debate is critical to improving monitoring programs, as it is for advancing any form of credible science.

EMAP

Because of increasing pressure in the US government for 'measuring for environmental results' (Reilly 1989), discussion started in 1988, and in 1990 the US Environmental Protection Agency (EPA) created EMAP, the Environmental Monitoring and Assessment Program in its Office of Research and Development (ORD) (Messer *et al.* 1991; McDonald *et al.* 2004). This large-scale monitoring program, designed to cover the entire USA, was formulated largely because of the need for large-scale environmental information on trends in the condition of ecological resources ranging from forests and agroecosystems to lakes, rivers and streams (Stevens 1994). The consequences of the absence of such data on the number and percentage of acidified lakes and streams became evident during the 'acid rain wars' (Likens 1992) of the 1980s in the USA. The EMAP was the brainchild of Dr Rick Linthurst, an enthusiastic and forward-thinking employee of the EPA, who had been heavily involved in the acid rain issue. The emphasis on measuring for results that could be applied, the experience with acid rain policy, and the broad scope of the program meant that EMAP was born already carrying a heavy mantle of bureaucracy.

The EMAP was described as a series of '*research programs to develop tools to monitor and assess the status and trends of the nation's ecological resources*' (www.epa.gov/emap). Although these are laudable objectives, we believe there are some substantial problems with the configuration and operation of EMAP.

Lack of focused questions and a conceptual model

The general objectives that drove the EMAP monitoring networks from the beginning were:

- 'To estimate current status, extent, changes, and trends in indicators of the Nation's ecological resources on a regional basis with known confidence';
- 'To monitor indicators of pollutant exposure and habitat condition, and to seek correlative relationships between human-induced stresses and ecological condition that identify possible causes of adverse effects', and
- 'To provide periodic statistical summaries and interpretive reports on ecological status and trends to the EPA Administrator and the public.' (Messer *et al.* 1991).

Although these objectives were vague, Messer *et al.* (1991) stated that EMAP was designed ' *to answer critical questions for policy and decision-makers and the public ...*'. Examples of the more detailed questions included:

- 'What is the current extent and location of our ecological resources (e.g. estuaries, lakes, forests, and wetlands) and how are they distributed geographically?'
- 'What percentages of the resources appear to be adversely affected by pollutants and other man-induced environmental stress, and in which regions are the problems most severe or widespread?'

- 'Which resources are degrading, where, and at what rate?'
- 'What are the relative patterns and magnitudes and the most likely causes of adverse effects?'
- 'Are the proportions of adversely affected ecosystems improving as expected in response to control and mitigation programs?'

These still rather vague questions became more specific for each category as the program evolved. The EMAP and its successors were able to answer some of these questions for coastal waters, lakes, and wadeable streams, and are in the testing stage for doing so for large rivers and wetlands (www.epa.gov/owow/monitoring/nationalsurveys.html).

The EMAP program was not initiated around a formal conceptual model although many scientists and consultants had been employed to help think through the development of the initial program, particularly the statistical design. Because of the absence of a conceptual model, EMAP attempted to monitor a very large number of environmental entities, a 'laundry list', of 'sentinel' species, 'keystone' species and a 'suite of indicators' plus numerous abiotic variables in a large number of natural resources, both terrestrial and aquatic, all with an elaborate statistical design for detecting spatial and temporal trends in these variables (e.g. McDonald *et al.* 2004). EMAP developed an 'Indicator Development Strategy', which focused on 'physical stressors', 'chemical stressors' and 'biological stressors' (Messer *et al.* 1991). The EMAP strategy was to identify and measure suites of indicators in all categories for each ecosystem type. The suite of response indicators was planned to reflect any actual adverse effects of both anticipated and unanticipated stressors, e.g. new pollutants. The focus on biotic indicators to assess condition, rather than on environmental conditions, was rather unusual at the time, but reflected the goals of EMAP.

Statistical design

One of the strengths, yet major problems with EMAP was its elaborate and rigid statistical design, which we believe was based on an unrealistically designed set of polygon-shaped spatial units. EMAP planned to focus on 'the development of unbiased statistical sampling frameworks.' Moreover, EMAP stated that, 'Probability-based sampling within a statistical survey design … provides the only unbiased estimate of the condition on an aquatic resource over a large geographic area from a small number of samples.' (McDonald *et al.* 2004). The return interval for sampling was every four years. Nevertheless, a main justification for these polygon-shaped, spatial units was that they would evenly cover the curved surface of the

Earth. A systematic grid of sampling points was established across the USA and continental shelf forming the basis for regional sampling at about 12 500 points in the contiguous 48 US States; each point was approximately 27 km apart in a triangular grid (Messer *et al.* 1991). After about 1994, EMAP focused on the value of the probability-based survey designs rather than the value of the hexagonal-grid design.

Management relevance

Although EMAP has operated during the past 18 years, relatively few 'State of the Environment' reports have been issued (www.epa.gov/roe/), but the EMAP surveys did contribute to these reports. As far as we can determine, there are five indicators in the recent State of the Nation's Ecosystems report (The Heinz Center 2008) based on EMAP. Thus, its relevance for advising the nation about environmental issues appears to have been significant in some areas, but overall rather limited given the size and expectations of the program. This reporting is in strong contrast to the 'Report Card' system of Moreton Bay in Queensland (see below), in which management assessments are made annually.

Loss of leadership

Even though Linthurst continued to be a strong champion for the EMAP program as Associate Director for Ecology at one of EPA's National Research Laboratories after he left his post as head of EMAP in 1996, in reality the passionate leader and champion for funding was lost and the program became immersed in the federal bureaucracy of the EPA. The EMAP program suffered from leadership instability with a string of directors (eight thus far) throughout its history. Additionally, with the change in federal administrations in the mid-1990s, EMAP's $43 million/year budget was reduced to $23 million/year with over half of that directed to a new competitive grants program.

Partnerships

Clearly, the EMAP program was trying to do the right thing with many viable partnerships including a variety of other federal agencies, state agencies and native tribes, which greatly expanded its already very substantial source of funding from the US Government. The goal of EMAP from the beginning was to integrate data from all of these networks (Messer *et al.* 1991), which was laudable, but in practice was not very successful.

According to EPA's 2009 Annual Performance Plan and Congressional Justification, EMAP was to be 'decreased' in 2009 as the national aquatic

---

BOX 4.3 EMAP REJOINDER

The EMAP was a major monitoring program in the USA, but it also was a monitoring research and development program as part of the EPA's Office of Research and Development. As such, it attempted to bring new approaches to monitoring at large, spatial scales. The statistical approach developed by EMAP has been adopted and endorsed by EPA's Office of Water (Coastal Condition Reports; Wadeable Streams Assessments and National Lakes Assessment; www.epa.gov/owow/monitoring/nationalsurveys.html). Despite what we believe to be shortcomings in a long-term monitoring program based on our criteria for success, we acknowledge EMAP's contributions to the development of environmental monitoring and particularly assessment protocols. It may not be obvious to readers from what we have written, but there were questions generated at the beginning, although we feel these questions were not as focused and scientifically rigorous as we would have liked to guide a massive program such as EMAP. The questions were general and directed at only management assessments. The EPA established performance measures in its Strategic Plan under the Government Performance Results Act for streams and coastal waters based on EMAP-designed surveys. The goal is to extend these measures to lakes and large rivers in the future.

It was contended that a conceptual model had been proposed for the EMAP monitoring program (see Figure 1 in Messer *et al.* 1991), but we have reservations about this model for several reasons. The primary one is because it is based on three categories of what we believe are indirect environmental indicators: response indicators, exposure indicators and stress indicators. We consider that using indicators instead of direct measures is not only problematic, but this approach falls short of using a broad, conceptual framework to guide understanding of ecosystem function that we propose as being critical in driving successful monitoring efforts (see Chapter 1).

---

surveys were to be transferred to other program offices, state administrations and native tribes, but with EMAP oversight and support. In reality, there was no more research into the design of monitoring, and ORD tended to view monitoring *per se* as outside of its mission.

NEON/TERN

Web address: www.neoninc.org; http://ncris.innovation.gov.au/Capabilities/Pages/TERN.aspx

This case study outlines two major research programs designed to help establish infrastructure for long-term ecological research and monitoring.

The research programs are the National Ecological Observatory Network (NEON) and the Terrestrial Environmental Research Network (TERN). They were initiated by the US National Science Foundation (NSF) and the Australian Department of Innovation, Industry, Science and Research, respectively. Currently, NEON is being planned and will be operated and maintained by a not-for-profit corporation called NEON Inc., although it is funded by the National Science Foundation. Both programs are funded from accounts that have traditionally been used to support the construction of expensive facilities for the physical sciences, such as large telescopes for astronomy. The US source of this funding comes from a special NSF program called Major Research Equipment and Facilities Construction (MREFC).

The NEON and TERN programs have, in many ways, remarkably similar recent histories even though they are in different countries. The NEON and TERN programs have been characterised by protracted discussions about what infrastructure should be funded (more than nine years of formal discussions during development of NEON), extensive and repeated consultations among large bodies of scientists about an appropriate way for the programs to proceed, considerable complication of the funding process, and the eventual disengagement and disenfranchisement of many people in the scientific communities of both nations. The procurement of infrastructure to support environmental research and monitoring is important and useful, but we believe there are problems with both schemes.

Lack of scientifically tractable questions, conceptual models or a priori predictions

Neither NEON nor TERN was driven from the start by testable and readily tractable scientifically based questions. There was no conceptual model associated with any of the funding, nor any *a priori* predictions about how the ecosystems where the infrastructure will be established might respond to environmental change or management interventions, other than in the most general terms. The three overarching questions for NEON as posted on the website in early 2009 are: (1) How are ecosystems across the United States affected over time by changes in climate, land use and invasive species? (2) How do biogeochemistry, biodiversity, hydroecology and biotic structure and function interact with changes in climate, land use and invasive species across the nation? (3) How do these feedbacks vary with ecological context and scale over time?

Like the NEON program, TERN is underpinned by vague questions. These include: (1) How does natural and human-induced change, both short- and long- term interact to alter ecosystem structure and function including remedial and mitigation measures? (2) How does biotic structure vary and be both a cause and consequence of ecological fluxes and energy? (3) What is the outcome for the net terrestrial CO_2 sink of the competing effects of CO_2 fertilisation, declining water availability, global warming, changing nutrient dynamics and disturbance by impacts? (4) How do altered community structure and ecosystem dynamics affect ecosystem services? (5) How can decision support systems, modelling complex processes, lead to mitigation and/or remedial measures based on human behaviour? (6) Which human actions influence the frequency and magnitude of change, or form of disturbance regimes across ecosystems, and conversely which human actions are required to mitigate or remediate degradation?

In essence, it appears that the 'real' questions for the work undertaken in the NEON and TERN programs are being posed **after** the money has been allocated, like unfortunately so much of ecological science. Therefore, in many respects, we believe the science is being done backwards.

In response to concerns and various controversies within the scientific community, especially regarding the source of the large amount of funding required by NEON, a committee was formed by the US National Academy of Sciences/National Research Council (NAS/NRC) to study the problems. This committee (Tilman 2003) endorsed the concept of NEON, but called for a 'refined focus and more detailed plan for implementation', and identified six 'Grand Challenges' in environmental biology to guide the overall effort. These were biodiversity; biogeochemical cycles; climate change; ecology and evolution of infectious diseases; invasive species, and land and habitat use. NEON planners have now identified a seventh grand challenge: invasive species (Schimel *et al.* 2009).

The NEON program has been in the discussion/formulation stage for a decade. Recently, there has been an attempt to generate detailed questions to drive the overall effort (Schimel *et al.* 2009). The NAS/NRC grand challenges report was an attempt to contribute in this regard and other efforts are now being made to generate guiding questions (see special issue of the journal *Frontiers in Ecology and the Environment*, Volume 6, 2008). Nevertheless, it is fair to state that infrastructure design and construction is and has been the major driving force for NEON from the beginning.

Focus on infrastructure

The primary focus of NEON and to a lesser extent TERN, has been on built infrastructure or equipment. Indeed, the NEON and TERN programs have arisen, in part, because some advocates believed that large equipment grants typical in the physical sciences should be extended into the ecological and environmental sciences. However, some disciplines like biodiversity conservation are markedly different than the physical sciences. Thus, while equipment is undoubtedly important in facilitating long-term research and monitoring, the importance of trained, dedicated people is equally important. We believe that it is vital to recognise the criticality of on-the-ground measurements by people, especially for the measurement of many elements of the biota. We have no doubt that exciting new insights can be gained from large and sophisticated equipment such as from flux towers. Such equipment can represent a very powerful tool for ecological studies. However, as we outline in Chapter 2, there can be serious statistical and experiment design issues (e.g. pseudo-replication) associated with expensive equipment that is a one-off, or for which only a small number can be purchased. There also are limitations in the spatial and temporal inferences that can be made from such equipment at a single site or from a small number of sites in countries the size of the USA and Australia. There also can be limitations to conclusions drawn about environmental impacts from measurements at a few sites. Finally, with a strong focus on infrastructure and questions posed post hoc (after the infrastructure has been established), there is a real danger that the two are mis-matched. That is, the infrastructure cannot be used to address the key questions that need to be answered. On the positive side, there is a strong commitment for broad geographic (continental) coverage of the infrastructure, which would be necessary to address large-scale problems such as climate change.

In a recent attempt to resolve this problem in NEON, mobile or 'relocatable' units are being planned for each of the 20 ecoclimatic 'domains' selected for study. We also appreciate that the NEON process identified 20 domains based on a sophisticated statistical analysis of climatic state variables and wind vectors. This was a valuable design effort, but in our opinion would have been even more valuable if preceded by a process of setting questions at the beginning or of integrating questions with the design.

Governance structure

NEON and TERN are supervised by a committee or board, although at the time of writing this book, the Board of TERN had not been appointed. The NEON board of directors, including a CEO, has 15 members, as well as a Project Manager. A large board is understandable given the very large amount of funding involved in both programs (some hundreds of millions of US dollars to be spent during the next 30 years in infrastructure and

BOX 4.4 NEON REJOINDER

There have been numerous and long-standing concerns from scientists, both inside and outside of the planning structure for NEON, but primarily about the fact that the focus on costly infrastructure was not driven at the outset by scientifically tractable questions. Nevertheless, as the long-term planning debate is coming to an end after a decade, many scientists have come to believe that it is better to have this new infrastructure than not have it. We agree! But we re-iterate that we would not want to see the funding for NEON infrastructure lead to the demise of other important ecological programs. Also, it is reasonable to believe that scientists will force a positive evolution toward the development of good questions that drives good ecological science when using this infrastructure, i.e. viable questions undoubtedly will be formulated by the user community after the infrastructure is in place and the reality of writing competitive grant proposals in a tight funding environment takes over. As we have argued above, however, it is much more efficient and scientifically sound to develop questions from the beginning. It is important to point out that NEON has not yet begun, so how all of this plays out in the future is unknown, but NEON will provide critical insights about the establishment and success of major monitoring programs. From our point-of-view there has been a strong commitment from the beginning for a broad, geographical (continental) coverage by NEON's infrastructure. This broad coverage will be vital for tackling emerging, large-scale environmental problems such as climate change.

possibly $50 million/year in operation costs for NEON). Some 55 'member' institutions, mostly universities, had signed on in support of the NEON effort in 2008. However, this structure has the potential to become problematic as Strayer *et al.* (1986) suggest that it is not good to do science by committee. Rather, we and they argue that leadership and appropriate leadership succession (see Chapter 5) by one or two key individuals is essential to making programs work over the truly long term (see Strayer *et al.* 1986).

Like all of our case studies in this section of the book, we believe that the NEON and TERN programs have been well intentioned and genuinely aimed at attempting to improve long-term ecological research and monitoring. Despite what we consider to be serious problems, we believe there are valuable aspects of both programs. The NEON and TERN programs have provided new sources of funding and promoted new collaborative efforts among scientists in often quite different disciplines and who may never have previously worked together. In addition, hopefully the newly built infrastructure may prove to be valuable for generating new scientific insights. In the case of TERN, there will be oversight for some long-term research and monitoring activities through a new Brisbane-based Australian Centre for Ecological Analysis and Synthesis (modelled, in part, on the National Centre for Ecological Analysis and Synthesis in Santa Barbara, California, USA). It will be instructive to track the effectiveness of that institution in guiding long-term research and monitoring in Australia.

Gauging success

NEON and TERN are very large initiatives and we believe it will be important to learn how success of these programs is gauged. Because of their bureaucratic structures, it may be that program success for NEON and TERN will be measured by expenditure on infrastructure; i.e. did we spend the money and buy what we said we would buy? In many respects, this is different to most traditional science in which success is gauged more by the kinds of scientific discoveries that are made.

THE EFFECTIVE

Rothamsted

Web address: www.rothamsted.ac.uk

It is not possible to write a book about long-term ecological research and monitoring without including arguably the most famous, and certainly the most long-running project of all; Rothamsted in England. Research at Rothamsted is conducted at two sites, one at Harpenden in Hertfordshire and a second near Bury St Edmunds in Suffolk. Rothamsted was established in 1834 and is the oldest active agricultural research station in the world (Rothamsted Research 2009). The two founders of Rothamsted, John Lawes and Henry Gilbert, established nine field experiments between 1843 and 1856 and only one of these was abandoned (in 1878). The remaining eight experiments continue to this day (Rothamsted Research 2006). Some of the classic experiments have been modified over time to address new questions or to add further treatments, as would be appropriate under the Adaptive Monitoring paradigm we describe in Chapter 3.

Considerable long-term monitoring has been conducted at Rothamsted and some of the world's truly classical experiments have been done there (Rothamsted Research 2006). They span studies of the effects of fertiliser application on crop yields, methods of crop improvement, pest resistance to agricultural chemicals and long-term changes in soil fertility

Figure 4.3 Aerial view of agricultural treatments at Rothamsted, England. (Copyright Rothamsted Research)

associated with different cropping systems. One of the most extraordinary studies resulted from analyses of levels of radioactivity from immaculately archived samples gathered over many years. These provided values for 'pre-atomic' baselines or background estimates of radioactivity for comparison with samples from the post-atomic era.

There are many reasons for the successes of the work at Rothamsted and we briefly summarise some of them below.

Well-defined questions
The classical experiments at Rothamsted (Rothamsted Research 2006), as well as the many subsequent studies conducted there are motivated by well-articulated and testable research questions about sustainable agriculture.

Statistical design
The work at Rothamsted is characterised by outstanding experimental design that reflects the value of scientists and statisticians working collaboratively. In many ways, the experiments at Rothamsted were the birth of

Figure 4.4 Archiving samples at Rothamsted, England. (Copyright Rothamsted Research)

modern statistics with luminaries such as RA Fischer being responsible for analysing major datasets gathered there and subsequently articulating key principles of experimental design and statistical analyses (Salsburg 2001). Notably, RA Fischer identified a number of substantial design issues from the first decades of experimentation at Rothamsted. These were addressed in subsequent studies such as through the application of what were then novel approaches like replication and randomisation (Salsburg 2001). The Lawes Agricultural Trust, which provides some of the financial support for the work at Rothamsted, also maintains support for the sophisticated and widely used statistical package GENSTAT.

Long-term financial stability

Access to ongoing funding has been part of the success of the Rothamsted research. In 1889, John Lawes established a Trust with £100 000 to fund the ongoing agronomic experiments. This endowment is administered by trustees and a trust committee.

Leadership

Long-term stable leadership lies at the core of the work at Rothamsted. John Lawes worked at Rothamsted for 50 years. Since then, subsequent directors have typically had long tenures.

Adaptive Monitoring

Work at Rothamsted has been long term, but nevertheless was highly responsive to new issues of management relevance. New questions have been posed in response to the insights gained from earlier findings, but these have not breached the integrity of the initial experiments. Therefore, existing projects have evolved and new ones have been instigated. This approach is highly congruent with the Adaptive Monitoring framework we describe in Chapter 3. For example, current work at Rothamsted include studies of genetically modified crops, carbon sequestration and climate change (Rothamsted Research 2009), topics that could not have even been comprehended by the initial founders of the work 175 years ago. Obviously the evolution of existing projects, coupled with new ones add considerably to the overall breadth and importance of work at Rothamsted and the body of knowledge resulting from the efforts at Rothamsted.

Moreton Bay Waterways and Catchment Partnership

(name change in 2006 to South East Queensland Healthy Waterways Partnership)

Web address: www.healthywaterways.org; http://www.ehmp.org

Moreton Bay is a large embayment in south-eastern Queensland, which borders the city of Brisbane and other urban areas, receiving drainage through the Brisbane, Logan, Pine, Caboolture and other smaller rivers from a catchment of some 22 000 km^2. Human population in the Brisbane area is 1.6 million with growth rates faster than anywhere else in Australia (10–13% per annum) (Skinner *et al.* 1998; Abal *et al.* 2005). Indeed, the population of the area is growing at an estimated rate of 1000 people each week, making it one of the fastest growing regions in the world (Skinner *et al.* 1998). Moreton Bay is an important marine environment, supporting many significant ecosystems, including extensive mangrove forests and

Figure 4.5 Caboolture River. (Photo courtesy of South East Queensland Healthy Waterways Partnership)

seagrass meadows, important marine mammal and other vertebrate populations (e.g. Chilvers *et al.* 2005), as well as an active seafood, recreational and tourist economy.

The management of Moreton Bay represents a substantial challenge not only because of its environmental values and large and rapidly increasing human population, but also because (**1**) the Bay supports commercial fisheries and recreational fishing; (**2**) it is a major shipping lane to national and international destinations and there are many associated industrial developments; (**3**) there is a high catchment to estuary ratio (14:1), with substantial discharges from numerous sub-catchments, particularly during large flood events, which are common in the area, and (**4**) there can be long residence times for pollutants in some parts of the bay (~200 days) (Chilvers *et al.* 2005).

In an effort to deal with the myriad environmental challenges associated with the management of Moreton Bay, such as increased nitrogen and phosphorus loading from sewage treatment discharge and stormwater runoff, sediment from growing urban centers and agricultural area, installation of upstream dams and dredging downstream (see Dennison and Abal 1999), the Moreton Bay Waterways and Catchments Partnership was established (Moreton Bay Waterways and Catchments

Figure 4.6 Press cuttings showing key environmental issues associated with the management of Moreton Bay near Brisbane, Australia.

Partnership 2003; Moreton Bay Waterways and Catchments Partnership 2004). Under the auspices of the partnership, the environmental condition of more than 250 estuarine and marine sites is monitored bimonthly, and some 135 freshwater sites are sampled mostly on a monthly basis (Moreton Bay Waterways and Catchments Partnership 2003; Moreton Bay Waterways and Catchments Partnership 2004). The total cost for this monitoring and reporting program is about $A3 million per year. Environmental management of Moreton Bay is based on rigorous research and monitoring, which is supported by the Partnership guiding the Adaptive Management approach. Annual 'report cards' are produced for the numerous catchments, estuaries and marine areas that comprise the Moreton Bay region (e.g. Moreton Bay Waterways and Catchments Partnership 2004; Ecosystem Health Monitoring Program 2008). Major problems that need to be addressed (for example stream-bank stabilisation or the need for sewage or industrial waste treatment) are identified and remediation programs are implemented in response. Significant improvements have been made; e.g. the reduction of the sewage plume at the mouth of the Brisbane River, and major reductions in the levels of nitrogen in the waterways.

The waterways and catchment partnership in Moreton Bay is an excellent model that demonstrates ways of using targeted monitoring programs and long-term ecological and hydrological research. The research and monitoring are based on management questions focused on improving management practices and environmental conditions, and incorporate the complexity of environmental and management issues to be tackled (O'Neill 2008). We believe there are a number of features which are pivotal to the success of this program.

Questions with management relevance
The research and especially the monitoring is driven by diverse questions with management relevance, such as how much would the loading of nutrients and sediment need to be reduced to improve the water quality and general environmental condition of Moreton Bay, and how could this be measured? This relevance occurs, in part, because the integrated study deals with pressing environmental problems that are highly pertinent to large numbers of people who, at the same time, are aggressive stakeholders in Moreton Bay and its catchment. The work has led to a demonstrable improvement in environmental conditions in Moreton Bay and hence it has a proven track record of success and management relevance.

Partnerships

The work in the Moreton Bay area has been built on strong partnerships forged between key stakeholders. The project is truly cross-disciplinary and links some of the best hydrologists and limnologists in the world to engineers, resource managers, policy-makers, politicians and the general public. In fact, some of the early topics for scientific study were suggested by the public (Dennison and Abal 1999). A key feature of the Moreton Bay Study was the functional interaction between scientific research and the development of a Water Quality Strategy.

High visibility

The Moreton Bay partnership is highly visible to politicians, the general public and resource managers. It has some strong and highly articulate advocates and produces a readily accessible and interpretable annual 'report card' on changes in environmental conditions in Moreton Bay (Ecosystem Heath Monitoring Program 2008). This report card has proven to be a politically powerful management tool. Extensive briefings occur prior to the issue of the 'report card', and the grades given receive much media attention. More often than not, a politician's future depends on the grade given in the report card for the environmental condition of the politician's jurisdiction.

Credibility and design

Some two to three years were invested in the design of this program by an independent group of scientists, engineers and managers before the program was initiated. As a result, the program was developed with a high degree of rigor and scientific integrity.

Strongly linked monitoring and management

High-quality environmental monitoring is a fundamental part of the Moreton Bay integrated Waterways and Catchments Partnership (Moreton Bay Waterways and Catchments Partnership 2003). The outcomes of the monitoring are reported in a transparent and readily interpretable way (e.g. Moreton Bay Waterways and Catchments Partnership 2004) and this has led to demonstrable changes in management practices, the development of new infrastructure to improve management practices, and enhanced environmental conditions (South East Queensland Healthy Waterways Partnership 2007). Ongoing and continuous review of the research and monitoring program, in response to new problems and questions, have been critical to maintaining a successful design and implementation (D Tarte, pers.comm.). This approach is consistent with our Adaptive Monitoring paradigm outlined in Chapter 3.

The Hubbard Brook Ecosystem Study

Web address: www.hubbardbrook.org

On 1 June 1963, what was to become the long-term research and monitoring program of the Hubbard Brook Ecosystem Study, was initiated. This long-term study has focused on the ecological, hydrological and biogeochemical dynamics of forest and associated aquatic ecosystems of the Hubbard Brook Experimental Forest in the White Mountains of New Hampshire, USA. Applying a medical analogy where the chemistry of blood and urine is used to evaluate human health, it was proposed at the beginning of this study that the chemistry of stream water, draining a complex watershed-ecosystem could be used to evaluate ecosystem function. The following is taken from the first proposal to the National Science Foundation in 1962, entitled, 'Hydrologic-mineral cycle interaction in a small watershed' by F Herbert Bormann and Gene E Likens.

'Given the basic abiotic and biotic complexity of land, the phenomena of succession and retrogression, a multiplicity of managerial goals, and a desire for more efficient use of the land, it is obvious that some theoretical framework upon which we can assemble and interrelate these diverse components is a necessity.

The ecosystem concept provides this framework [... and] may be visualised as a series of components such as species populations, organic debris, available nutrients, primary and secondary minerals, and atmospheric gases, linked together by food webs, nutrient flow, and energy flow. Knowledge of these components and the links involved, leads to an understanding of the interrelationships within the systems and of the ramifications of any manipulation applied at any point in the system.

Boundaries of an ecosystem are often defined to meet the pragmatic needs of the investigator. But once this definition is made, the ecosystem may be visualised as being connected to the surrounding biosphere by a system of inputs and outputs.

[...] Nutrient cycles are strongly geared, at many points, to the hydrologic cycle. As a consequence, measurement of nutrient input and output requires simultaneous measurement of hydrologic input and output.

An investigation is proposed into the absolute rates of mineral generation, withdrawal and circulation within a small ecosystem. The experimental area selected is a small watershed in the Hubbard Brook Experimental Forest (HBEF) in West Thornton, New Hampshire.'

Some basic approaches and objectives identified in this first proposal included (1) the need for a conceptual model to guide research (see Figure 4.10); (2) the value of the ecosystem concept; (3) the need for watershed-scale, experimental studies with a reference ('control'); (4) the evaluation of the critical relation between 'mineral cycles' and hydrology; (5) the need for the perspective of long-term data; (6) the realisation that budgets (mass balances) can provide diagnostic tools for analysing complicated ecosystems; (7) the value of archiving samples for future use, and (8) the need to relate scientific research to land and water management issues.

Some terms and concepts in this early proposal that are changed or no longer used include: 'mineral cycles' which has become 'nutrient' or 'element cycles', since strictly speaking, *minerals* don't cycle; 'man's' has become 'human's' effects; and the 'climax' concept for ultimate vegetation development is no longer used.

The original research team included F Herbert Bormann, plant ecologist; Gene E Likens, aquatic ecologist; Noye M Johnson, geologist; and Robert S Pierce, soil scientist. Bormann, Likens and Johnson were faculty members at Dartmouth College in Hanover, NH, and Pierce was Project Leader for the US Forest Service in charge of the Hubbard Brook Experimental Forest.

A brief story provides an example of the critical role that serendipity played in the success of the early, long-term research and monitoring program at the Hubbard Brook Experimental Forest. Many peers were sceptical that this first proposal represented a viable approach for the study of large, complicated ecosystems, because no-one had done that kind of study on the scale of an entire watershed. To do the extensive chemical analyses (none of the original scientists were trained as chemists) the Hubbard Brook team had to develop and test their own procedures, and there was much to be done. Noye Johnson argued that the focus should be on calcium, magnesium, sodium, potassium because as a geologist trained in the midwestern USA, his geochemical view of the world depended upon carbon dioxide and carbonate. Likens and Bormann believed that phosphorus and nitrogen would be extremely important ecologically, but the team went along with Johnson's approach as a way to start. Even so, how to do it? It was planned to use an EDTA titration, which is a laborious, wet-chemistry method for measuring base cations (calcium, magnesium, sodium, potassium) in solution. This dilemma had been discussed with various colleagues when Bormann learned that a recently graduated PhD student from Rutgers University, Clarence Grant, had just joined the faculty of the University of New Hampshire in Durham. Bormann and Likens visited Grant and spent about an hour telling him what they planned to do, including all the chemistry. Grant was an excellent soil chemist, and was highly sceptical, if not discouraging, of the possibility of success! Just as Bormann and Likens were leaving Grant's office, Grant said, '*I remember something that came in the mail the other day, a flyer about a new instrument that might be helpful to you.*' He looked through a pile of papers and pulled out the flyer. '*Here it is, a new instrument called the . . . atomic absorption spectrophotometer.*' This instrument had been developed by a scientist in the Commonwealth Scientific and Industrial Research Organisation (CSIRO) in Australia largely to avoid interferences in the measurement of base cations, when analysing blood and urine.

Returning home to Dartmouth College, Likens called the Perkin-Elmer Corporation in Norwalk, Connecticut, and promptly bought one of these new instruments (Model 303) on a grant from the National Science Foundation. It was stamped 'No. 15' on the back, and was the first one

Figure 4.7 Ice on Mirror Lake in the Hubbard Brook Valley. (Photo by Donald C Buso)

Figure 4.8 Gauging weir at Hubbard Brook Experimental Forest. (Photo by Gene E Likens)

Figure 4.9 Rainfall and snowfall measurement site at Hubbard Brook Experimental Forest. (Photo by Donald C Buso)

purchased or used outside a medical facility in the United States. As it turned out, this instrument made the Hubbard Brook Ecosystem Study possible. It is probably fair to state that there would not have been a long-term Hubbard Brook Ecosystem Study without the availability of that tool at just that time.

This was a serendipitous event: a phone call, a meeting that caught the fancy of someone with additional knowledge, all making the research project so much more enriched and productive. And this early development of the Hubbard Brook Ecosystem Study was not dependent on buying people's time or services or some tool *per se*; instead it developed through a question, cooperation, enthusiasm and especially, trust among the interested investigators.

The Hubbard Brook Ecosystem Study started in 1963 and has now been in continuous operation for 46 years. The US Forest Service had started hydro-meteorological measurements some eight years earlier. A large number of entities are now monitored on a continuing basis in the Hubbard Brook Valley including solar radiation; air, stream and lake temperature; precipitation amount and chemical content; air chemistry; stream water, including flow and chemical content; soil-water chemistry; forest population dynamics and biomass accumulation; litterfall; bird, salamander and snail populations, and a variety of limnological parameters in Mirror Lake, including ice in and ice out dates.

Experimental watershed-ecosystem manipulations in response to questions at the ecosystem scale have been a hallmark of the long-term research of the Hubbard Brook Ecosystem Study and several are ongoing including those addressing questions about forest harvest (clearcutting) and nutrient depletion from the effects of acid rain. Paired watershed-ecosystems provide a reference (Likens 1985a) for evaluating the long-term effects of the experimental manipulations.

The Hubbard Brook Ecosystem Study is a good example of long-term monitoring. There are a number of key characteristics of the work which have contributed to its success and major influence on many aspects of environmental management including its sustained productivity and integrity over a 46-year period (Likens 2004).

Well-defined questions and evolving questions

The Hubbard Brook Ecosystem Study has been driven by carefully formulated and scientifically tractable questions. These have continued to evolve to this day as new insights trigger new lines of inquiry. Indeed, over the years the steady stream of proposals submitted to agencies such as the

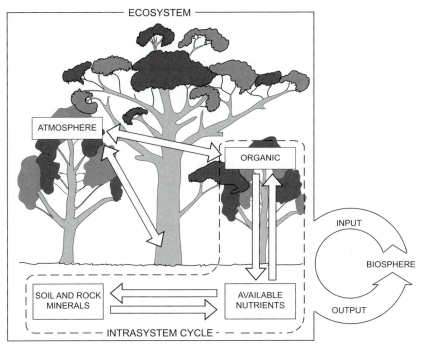

Figure 4.10 A conceptual model for biogeochemical relationships and input and output fluxes in a terrestrial ecosystem. (Redrawn from Bormann and Likens 1967, reprinted with permission from AAAS)

National Science Foundation needed to be driven by compelling questions to obtain ongoing funding in a very competitive, peer-review environment.

Conceptual model

The early development and continued use of a conceptual biogeochemical model (Figure 4.10) (Bormann and Likens 1967) to guide ecosystem research and analysis, helped to formulate new questions and helped to identify gaps in research directions. With time, this conceptual model became more complicated but still retained its usefulness in guiding thinking and research for the Hubbard Brook Ecosystem Study. This long-term usefulness was related in large part because of the biogeochemical focus of the Hubbard Brook Ecosystem Study. In 2004, a new model was developed and published (Groffman *et al.* 2004b). This model is more complicated than the one in Figure 4.10 in terms of entities and concepts included, but to-date its usefulness for guiding the thinking and activity of the Hubbard Brook Ecosystem Study has been limited.

Focus on scientific productivity and synthesis materials

The research at the Hubbard Brook Experimental Forest has been highly productive (see www.hubbardbrook.org). There are many important facets of this work and these are often intimately interlinked. Cross-fertilisation often leads to greater insights than would be apparent from consideration of the individual parts in isolation. Given this, a major feature has been the integration of results leading to synthesis books (Likens *et al.* 1977; Bormann and Likens 1979; Likens 1985a; Likens 1992; Likens and Bormann 1995; Winter and Likens 2009) and some 26 monographic treatments (e.g. Bormann *et al.* 1970; Likens *et al.* 1970; Fisher and Likens 1973; Marks 1974; Whittaker *et al.* 1974; Holmes *et al.* 1986; Likens *et al.* 1994; Likens *et al.* 1998; Likens *et al.* 2002; Fahey *et al.* 2005; Lovett *et al.* 2005; Groffman *et al.* 2006).

Demonstrated importance of long-term research

The Hubbard Brook Ecosystem Study has continued to highlight and nurture the concept of long-term studies (e.g. Likens *et al.* 1977; Bormann and Likens 1979; Likens 1992; Likens and Bormann 1995; Likens 2004; Holmes 2007; Siccama *et al.* 2007) even though it was often very difficult to maintain uninterrupted funding. For example, although the forest in south-facing catchments of the Hubbard Brook Experimental Forest appears green and robust, research conducted since 1965 is now indicating, surprisingly, that this forest is no longer accumulating biomass. It is now losing biomass as a result of increased mortality of dominant tree species, primarily sugar maple (*Acer saccharum*) because of loss of soil nutrients from the effects of acid rain, mobilisation of toxic aluminium and introduced pests and pathogens (Figure 4.11; Likens *et al.* 1998; Siccama *et al.* 2007; Likens and Franklin 2009). From a carbon sequestration perspective, it might be argued that this long-term record became interesting only after ~20 years of monitoring.

Collaboration

Long-term research and monitoring at the Hubbard Brook Experimental Forest has been characterised by strong research partnerships among scientists from the US Forest Service, the US Geological Survey, and numerous universities and research institutes who work cooperatively as part of a scientific team.

Field presence

Initially, a small, focused and dedicated team of senior researchers spent much time in residence, interacting together at the Hubbard Brook Experimental Forest (see Chapter 5). Currently, some 30 senior scientists and a

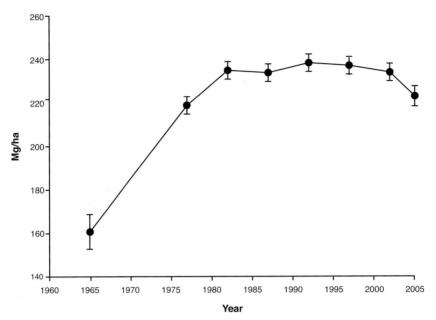

Figure 4.11 Changes in forest biomass over time at Hubbard Brook Experimental Forest, New Hampshire. (Modified from data of RH Whittaker, TG Siccama, J Battles and others)

large number of students and support staff work at the Hubbard Brook Experimental Forest. The long-term, competent, dedicated and enthusiastic support personnel have been central to the success of the Hubbard Brook Ecosystem Study (see also Chapter 2).

Careful use and calibration of field equipment

A feature of the biogeochemical monitoring at the Hubbard Brook Experimental Forest has been the use of analytical procedures that were neither changed nor replaced without first overlapping and comparing results from the 'long-term method' with those from a proposed new method. This approach avoided 'artifacts' in the long-term chemical record (Buso *et al.* 2000).

Deficiencies

In spite of the long-term successes of the Hubbard Brook Ecosystem Study, there are several deficiencies and problems. This long-term study is a 'one of a kind' in that it is not, and can not, be replicated, which is important in scientific research. Moreover, watershed-ecosystem manipulations can be subject to pseudoreplication (Hurlbert 1984), but this problem is alleviated by the paired-watershed approach and the long-term nature of the study. Nevertheless, sometimes results are so obvious that statistics are not necessary and may be a diversion (Likens 1992; DW Schindler 2005 pers.comm.). A related issue is the decreasing availability of undisturbed watershed-ecosystems for new experimental manipulation as watershed-ecosystems are used for long-term experimental manipulation (Likens 2004; Likens and Buso 2008).

Another issue is the increasing bureaucracy associated with running the research and monitoring program with increasing numbers of scientists from increasing numbers of institutions, which potentially adds to complicated interpersonal dynamics of interacting scientists, and fragmentation in focus of the study. Over the years, sustaining the funding necessary to continue the long-term monitoring has been very difficult, and currently is especially so given the tight funding environment for ecological research in the US.

Other problems include: extrapolation of detailed site results to larger areas and different ecoregions, and issues of leadership succession following the deaths of two of the founding leaders (Johnson in 1987; Pierce in 1993) and the retirement of a third (Bormann in 1992). Likens stepped down as co-director of the Hubbard Brook Ecosystem Study in 1990, although he continues to be very active in the study. Currently, Charles Driscoll and Tim Fahey are the principal investigators of the NSF-funded Long-Term Ecological Research (LTER) program initiated in 1988 at the Hubbard Brook Experimental Forest. The LTER program is now a major component of the overall Hubbard Brook Ecosystem Study. In response to growth and complexity of the Hubbard Brook Ecosystem Study, a new governance structure was initiated in 2004 (Groffman et al. 2004a). Peter Groffman currently chairs the Scientific Co-ordinating Committee in this governance structure.

The Central Highlands of Victoria, south-eastern Australia

Web address: http://fennerschool-research.anu.edu.au/cle

The wet montane ash eucalypt forests of the Central Highlands of Victoria are the focus of this case study (Figure 4.12). The study area comprises about one degree of latitude and longitude and lies approximately 100 km north-east of Melbourne, the second largest city in Australia. These are spectacular forests and support the tallest flowering plants in the world, with trees in old growth stands sometimes exceeding 100 m in height (Beale 2007). They are also important forests for (1) timber and pulpwood production; (2) biodiversity conservation – the distribution of the endangered

Figure 4.12 A stand of old growth mountain ash. The person in the mid-ground highlights both the size and height of the trees in this stand. (Photo by Esther Beaton)

Leadbeater's possum (*Gymnobelideus leadbeateri*) is virtually confined to stands of ash-type eucalypts; (3) the production of water to supply Melbourne; (4) human recreation, and (5) carbon storage (Keith *et al.* 2009).

The work in the Central Highlands of Victoria was initially established to quantify the factors influencing the distribution and abundance of arboreal marsupials throughout the ash-type forests (Smith and Lindenmayer 1988). A particular focus was on the nationally endangered Leadbeater's possum because (1) it was important to know where the species was most likely to occur to provide a spatial context for managing logging operations; (2) there were concerns about the potential impacts of logging operations on the species, and (3) arboreal marsupials are cavity-dependent animals and typically occupy trees that are 150 years or older. Logging operations alter the structure of forests and, in particular, reduce the abundance of cavity trees and significantly delay the time until new ones are recruited (Gibbons and Lindenmayer 2002). And, (4) There were community demands to develop approaches to mitigate logging effects on biodiversity (including Leadbeater's possum) and introduce new strategies to integrate wood production and conservation better in ash-type forests (Lindenmayer 2009).

The work commenced in 1983 and continues today. It has been led by a single investigator (David Lindenmayer) since that time. Since then, the research program in the Central Highlands of Victoria has grown to span several broad themes **(1)** from single species work to species assemblages research; **(2)** spatial patterns (e.g. forest cover and composition) to work on ecological processes (e.g. fire and tree fall); **(3)** empirical work to simulation modelling; **(4)** observational studies to manipulative experiments, and **(5)** ecological theory to applied ecological research (Lindenmayer 2009).

The study which formed the backbone of the work was a carefully designed and executed set of repeated animal and vegetation surveys at over 160 sites distributed widely in the Central Highlands of Victoria. The selection of the 160+ sites was guided by strong contrasts in a range of key environmental conditions. These included **(1)** logging and disturbance history: places that have recently been logged and regenerated versus others with no history of cutting; **(2)** topographic location and elevation: sites on steep slopes versus those on flat terrain, and **(3)** proximity to human disturbance: sites close to human habitation and those remote from it. There was spatial dispersion of sites to avoid geographical bias and extensive replication of sites within cells representing combinations of stratifying factors to quantify variability and ensure that results of subsequent statistical modelling of field data were robust. That initial study continues to provide the framework for a long-term monitoring study of animal population dynamics, the dynamics of vegetation structure and composition and the inter-linkages between the two (Lindenmayer *et al.* 2003). Key questions that have motivated the monitoring program have been:

- What are temporal patterns of animal abundance?
- What are the temporal patterns of abundance of large trees with hollows? These trees are primary nesting and denning sites for cavity-dependent animals, including Leadbeater's possum.
- What are the relationships between the abundance of trees with hollows and the occurrence of different species of arboreal marsupials?
- Do these relationships change as the number of trees with hollows declines over time?
- Are actual changes in populations of animals congruent with those forecast to occur as a consequence of declining populations of trees with hollows?

An early (and obvious) insight was that Leadbeater's possum did not exist in isolation from other animals, including other species of arboreal marsupials. Information on other species of arboreal marsupials was therefore needed to identify better where Leadbeater's possum did and did not occur and the underlying reasons for those patterns of occurrence.

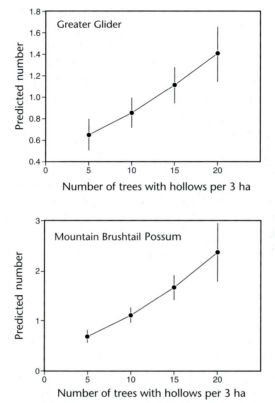

Figure 4.13 **Relationships between the probability of arboreal marsupials and the abundance of trees with hollows. (Redrawn from Lindenmayer *et al.* 1990c; Lindenmayer *et al.* 1991b; with permission from Elsevier)**

Hence, studies of a single species expanded to encompass other species and ultimately the entire assemblage of possums and gliders as well as many taxa from other groups such as birds and terrestrial mammals. The composition and structure of the forests strongly influence where these animals live (Lindenmayer *et al.* 1991b) and the research program expanded to include work on this topic. Habitat suitability is strongly shaped by the ecological process of disturbance and this made it essential to quantify the impacts of fires and logging on the stand structure and landscape composition (Lindenmayer and McCarthy 2002). Learning how to mitigate the impacts of human disturbance on forest biodiversity was therefore informed by (**1**) quantifying where species occurred; (**2**) why they occurred where they did, and (**3**) how disturbance dynamics influenced the key resources required by the target species of management concern. In

Figures 4.14 A. Marked standing tree. B. Collapsed tree. (Photos by David Lindenmayer)

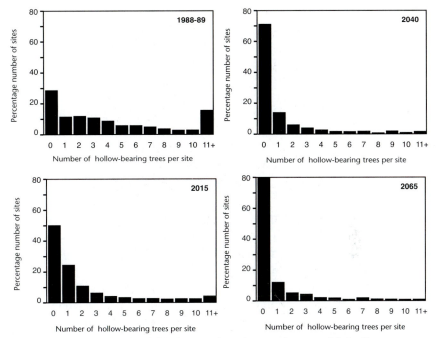

Figure 4.15 Projections of the future abundance of trees with hollows. (Lindenmayer *et al.* 1990a, with permission from Elsevier)

particular, how logging changed key attributes of stand structure and landscape composition and, in turn, how logging practices might be altered to reduce such impacts (Lindenmayer and Franklin 2002).

Research on arboreal marsupials at the long-term monitoring sites demonstrated highly significant relationships between the presence and abundance of arboreal marsupials and the abundance of trees with hollows on those sites (see below). Importantly, the performance of statistical models relating animal occurrence and the abundance of trees with hollows was examined with a new dataset comprising an additional 55 field sites. This work showed that the models performed well when tested in this way (Lindenmayer *et al.* 1994). Other studies identified a series of inter-related ecological mechanisms influencing these relationships: (**1**) Different species partition the hollow-tree resource and select trees with different characteristics (Lindenmayer *et al.* 1991c). (**2**) Different species rarely co-occur in the same tree (Lindenmayer *et al.* 1990b). (**3**) Each species of arboreal marsupial swaps regularly between den trees and typically uses between six and 20 different trees in a given year (Lindenmayer *et al.* 1996).

These factors mean that only those sites with many trees with hollows are likely to fulfill the requirements of most species of arboreal marsupials. This pattern, in turn, explains the highly significant relationships identified for animal presence and abundance and the abundance of trees with hollows in montane ash forests (Figure 4.13) (Lindenmayer 2009).

A 26-year study of over 1100 marked large trees with hollows revealed that the death and collapse of these trees is far outstripping the rate of recruitment of new ones. Predictions from these data indicate that there will be a chronic shortage of these trees throughout large parts of the montane ash forests for 50 or more years beyond 2050 (Figure 4.15) (Lindenmayer *et al.* 1990a; Lindenmayer *et al.* 1997; Lindenmayer and Wood 2009).

Given known relationships between the abundance of trees with hollows and the abundance of arboreal marsupials, data on the collapse of trees were used to make projections of future animal population decline for 50 years up until 2050 when new trees with hollows were predicted to begin being recruited (Figure 4.14). These projections show that all three key species modelled are forecast to undergo substantial declines in the coming 40 years (Figure 4.16). These projections have, in turn, been appropriate for making comparisons with actual data on animal population dynamics gathered from the long-term monitoring sites between 1990 and 2009. That is, projected changes have been compared with actual changes. The results of those comparisons have been instructive. To date, these data show that populations of Leadbeater's possum fluctuate substantially from year to year but no discernible trend signal for population increase or decrease is seen. Conversely, the greater glider has undergone a substantial decline, whereas the mountain brushtail possum has actually increased. These unexpected trends have forced a rethink of temporal changes in animal-habitat relationship and new work on social behaviour and patterns of tree use has commenced in an attempt to develop a better understanding of the results that have been obtained to date.

The work in the Central Highlands of Victoria has led to some valuable insights. It was some of the first research in Australia to rigorously quantify the impacts of conventional clearcut logging methods on forest vegetation structure, plant species composition and the response of animals such as Leadbeater's possum as well as other species of arboreal marsupial (Lindenmayer *et al.* 1990d; Lindenmayer 2009). For many years, forest management in Victoria was based on a simple assumption that wet eucalypt forests are almost exclusively even-aged as a result of stand-replacing wildfires. However, the work in the Central Highlands of

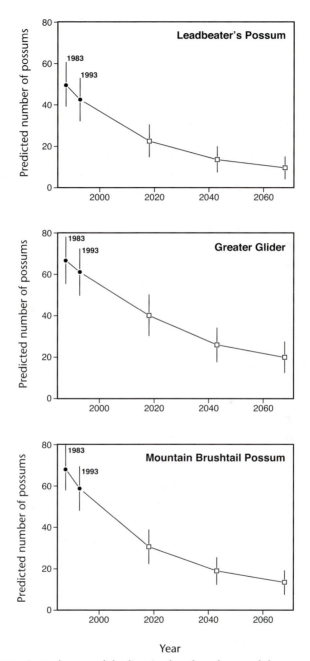

Figure 4.16 Projected rates of decline in the abundance of three species of cavity-dependent arboreal marsupials. (Redrawn from Lindenmayer *et al.* 1997)

Victoria showed that almost all old growth stands actually comprised dominant trees of multiple ages, changing the comprehension of how these forests function (Lindenmayer *et al.* 2000). Using empirical analysis based on extensive field data on vegetation, it was then demonstrated that random and deterministic influences of climate, terrain and other factors significantly influenced the development of multi-aged stands in particular parts of forest landscapes (Mackey *et al.* 2002). Such multi-aged forests are important because they support the highest diversity of arboreal marsupials (Lindenmayer *et al.* 1991b) as well as large numbers of species of other groups such as birds. Discoveries on old growth, multi-aged forest and patterns of natural disturbance resulted in the development of new perspectives on the impacts of post-disturbance salvage logging. It was shown that a combination of natural disturbance (fire) and human disturbance (post-fire salvage logging) could lead to cumulative effects more significant and more prolonged in their impacts than either kind of disturbance in isolation (Lindenmayer and Ough 2006). These new perspectives have led to new conservation management strategies within forests broadly designated for wood production, including greater regulation of where logging can and cannot take place, and limits on where post-fire salvage logging is permitted. It also led to the instigation of a replicated logging experiment in which greater levels of tree retention on cut sites, resulting in the eventual development of multi-aged forest and an expansion of suitable habitat for logging-sensitive species (Lindenmayer 2007).

The long-term studies and monitoring program in the Central Highlands of Victoria are characterised by some important features.

Stability
The same person has been the leader of the project over the past 26 years and has maintained the work even though there have been five major restructures of government agencies responsible for forest and conservation management in that time.

Expert statistical design
Four highly qualified professional statisticians have played pivotal roles in the research. They have been responsible for assisting in the framing of tractable scientific questions, the design of observational studies and experiments, conducting cutting-edge statistical analyses of complex datasets, the development of new statistical methods, and contributing to the ecological auditing of projects to determine whether field data collection should continue or if detailed analyses of data were appropriate.

BOX 4.5 POSTSCRIPT: FEBRUARY 2009 WILDFIRES

On 7 February 2009, major wildfires began burning throughout large parts of the Central Highlands of Victoria, as well as other parts of that State. They eventually became the worst fires in Australia's history with 173 lives lost and over 3000 homes destroyed. The fires also had an enormous impact on the long-term studies in the ash forests of the region and many sites were damaged as a result of the conflagration (Figure 4.17). However, it has been important to treat the fire as a new opportunity to learn about post-fire ecological recovery. The fires also have meant that the work in the Victorian forests has become an example of Adaptive Monitoring (*sensu* Chapter 3).

The February 2009 wildfires burned 64 of the 161 permanent field monitoring sites, although at varying severity (typically either very high severity or moderate severity). The forest at the time of the fire on the burned sites varied from old growth (>300 years) through to 20-year-old regrowth. Thus, differences in fire severity as well as differences in stand age at the time of disturbance, coupled with the past 26 years of previous work on the long-term monitoring sites, have provided an ideal background for a longitudinal study. This study has been designed to assess the responses of fauna and flora to fire of differing severity in relation to site history (stand age at the time of the 2009 fire) and pre-fire vegetation floristics and structure. Longitudinal studies of this type provide direct measures of change. This opportunity occurs because detailed longitudinal profiles of each site had been developed prior to the 2009 wildfires. This design will help overcome some of the significant limitations of many fire studies, which are post hoc and lack pre-fire data, thereby substantially limiting the inferences about fire impacts and post-fire recovery that can be made (Whelan 1995; Lindenmayer and Burgman 2005).

In mid-April 2009, as soon as access to the forest was permitted, work commenced re-measuring the vegetation and the vertebrate fauna at all 161 long-term monitoring sites (i.e. both burned and unburned). This research is planned to continue for many years into the future. This work is an example of Adaptive Monitoring because the wildfire intervention has demanded that new questions be answered. These questions include:

- What are the relationships between pre-fire plant and animal populations and post-fire population trajectories? How does burn severity influence these trajectories, for example, in terms of species richness, community composition, and populations of individual species? What are these relationships for nationally threatened species such as Leadbeater's possum?
- How are recovery trajectories influenced by initial conditions (stand age at the time of the 2009 fire), the severity of the 2009 fire, and the interaction of initial conditions and burn severity?

- Does burn severity and past fire history differentially influence certain kinds of species (e.g. functional groups of plants or particular guilds of arboreal marsupials and birds?) Are there particular sets of life history attributes common to species which increase vs decrease over time?
- Is there a well defined successional replacement of species within particular groups over time, as predicted by the habitat accommodation model (Fox 1982)?
- Are there landscape context effects? That is, is the recovery process at a site influenced by the extent of unburned and burned forest surrounding a site?
- How valid are a range of ecological theories and concepts associated with natural disturbance regimes such as Egler's (1954) initial conditions hypothesis, the intermediate disturbance hypothesis (Shiel and Burslem 2003), the biological legacies concept (*sensu* Franklin *et al.* 2000), and the vegetation mosaic hypothesis (Parr and Andersen 2006)?

Tractable approach to field research and monitoring

Although many studies have been completed over the 26-year history of work, each investigation has been characterised by careful posing of questions and the collection of a tractable set of covariates for subsequent

Figure 4.17 A stand of burned old growth forest following the February 2009 wildfires. The site is the same forest as shown prior to the fires in Figure 4.12. (Photo by David Lindenmayer)

analyses. There has never been a desire to 'monitor everything' by the 'laundry-list' method, nor has there been an assumption that Leadbeater's possum (nor any other species or group) was an indicator species for some other entity or species or group (Lindenmayer and Cunningham 1997).

Ongoing development of questions and research themes

The scope and breadth of work undertaken has grown over the period of the project. This directed growth has occurred because new insights and discoveries have prompted new questions and triggered new studies such as those of ecological recovery following the 2009 wildfire. These studies have been built around a framework of monitoring sites without compromising the integrity of that framework or the integrity of the long-term datasets being gathered. This approach has added greatly to the body of knowledge about the study region and created valuable cross-fertilisation between research themes and topics, thereby creating a better understanding of the forest patterns and ecological processes and the mechanisms that link them in ash-type eucalypt forests (Lindenmayer 2009).

High levels of scientific productivity

The research in the Central Highlands of Victoria has led to the publication of more than 165 scientific articles as well as five books. This productivity has helped establish the scientific credentials of the work and emphasised its value to policy-makers, resource managers and politicians.

Partnerships

Much of the work in the Central Highlands of Victoria has involved establishing working relationships between researchers and staff from government agencies responsible for forest management and wildlife conservation. This development of relationships has been done deliberately to ensure that the results of the work can be adopted in on-the-ground management practices. It also has been critical to the establishment of logging experiments designed to identify more environmentally sensitive silvicultural systems than traditional clearcutting. Large numbers of volunteers have been involved in some of the field-counting protocols and partnerships with community conservation groups have greatly assisted field data collection (Lindenmayer *et al.* 1991a).

Quality of on-the-ground staff

Part of the success of this project is due to very high quality field staff, working full-time in the forest to gather field data. These field staff also have been adept at data curation and database management.

Deficiencies

The work in the Central Highlands of Victoria has a number of weaknesses and problems. First, much of the initial work was based on quantifying patterns and far less emphasis was placed on the ecological processes or mechanisms giving rise to those patterns. Additional effort has been focused on rectifying this deficiency in the past decade, but a lot more work is required to address this problem. Second, the use of a tractable and explicit conceptual model that is at the core of the Adaptive Monitoring framework (see Chapter 3) and fundamental to the success of the Hubbard Brook Ecosystem Study (see above) was only very recently adopted in the Central Highlands of Victoria. Third, and typical of virtually all long-term monitoring, is funding. For many years the project was run using book royalties and other small and insecure sources of money. The work currently has five additional years of funding (to the end of 2014) and the future of the project following that date remains uncertain. A fourth deficiency has been that the initial study, which now forms the basis for the 26-year monitoring program of populations of arboreal marsupials, was an observational, retrospective investigation. Although it was carefully designed and implemented, these kinds of studies are less powerful for making inferences than traditional experiments and natural experiments. More recent work has been based around the implementation of true experiments (Lindenmayer 2007; Lindenmayer 2009) and innovative statistical approaches are being developed to link past observational work with more recently established experiments. Fifth, the leader of the long-term study has fallen victim to the modern problem of fragmentation of effort, ideas and time and is responsible for five other large-scale projects in south-eastern Australia. Hence, the focus on the long-term study in the Central Highlands of Victoria is not as acute as it should be. Sixth, there have been periods over the past 26 years where communication between researchers and resource managers and policy-makers has not been nearly as frequent as it should have been and this has led to such problems as logging of monitoring sites and other kinds of damage to experimental sites. Finally, although the Central Highlands of Victoria is part of an informal alliance of LTER sites in Australia, neither the data nor insights from the work have been drawn into the national State of the Environment Report series (State of the Environment Advisory Council 1996; State of the Environment Report 2001). This integration between environmental reporting and monitoring programs is an unresolved and vexed problem that we discuss further in Chapter 5.

BOX 4.6 THE CRAWFORD CAPER

With Bermuda as the last port of call, the ship *Crawford* arrived at the WHOI (Woods Hole Oceanographic Institution) pier on the afternoon of 19 March 1960, and quickly cleared customs and immigration with the usual New Bedford (Massachusetts) agents. When unloading was nearly finished, four Boston customs agents materialised to confiscate the booze that, by long-standing practice, cruise participants had been bringing home to the USA. More than 80 cases were confiscated, two personal vehicles were seized, and *Crawford* captain David Casiles was charged with allowing illegal importation. The ship *Chain,* due in three days later, was cryptically notified, and Captain Hiller put all the liquor aboard the ship in bond (for later seizure, as it turned out). *Crawford* was allowed to continue operating, although it was for a time officially the property of the US Customs (which assigned custody to Captain Casiles!). A three-person internal investigating committee determined that the liquor was not intended for commercial purposes, and a payment of $US4500 fine (contributed by those who had benefited from the contraband over the years) cleared Captain Casiles. New policies were put in place, but life with customs was made difficult for some time (modified from Cullen 2005). Ostensibly, a major justification for this 'rum run' route, was to monitor temperature and salinity profiles (T-S diagrams) in the ocean between Massachusetts to Bermuda. Although WHOI has done some of the most exemplary research and monitoring of the world's oceans, it seems to us that the results leading to this 'caper' qualifies as mindless monitoring of the 'ugly' type.

THE UGLY

We have chosen not to devote any significant space to 'The Ugly' category of monitoring in this book. Hopefully, there are very few examples! Let the one example we give in Box 4.6 suffice.

SUMMARY

In this chapter we have presented a series of case studies of long-term ecological research and monitoring programs. We have outlined what we believe to be problematic and effective monitoring. We believe there are sets of common problems with problematic programs and, conversely, a suite of features that characterise effective monitoring programs. To be fair, none of the effective programs are perfect nor do the problematic programs lack redeeming features.

In our view, the problematic programs generally have two or more of the following deficiencies: (1) A lack of well-defined scientifically tractable questions at the beginning of the effort. (2) The absence of a useful conceptual model. (3) No apparent experimental design or a poor experimental design. And, (4) 'Laundry lists' of attributes to be measured.

In contrast, effective long-term studies usually have two or more of the following features: (1) Well-defined and scientifically tractable questions. New questions are often posed as new insights are gained, but these do not breach the integrity of long-term research and monitoring. (2) Take advantage of serendipity (defined as keeping ones eyes, ears and mind open to new questions and then moving expeditiously to address them) in combination with Adaptive Monitoring to update and energise long-term research. Examples include those of analyses of radioactivity at Rothamsted and the discovery of acid rain at the Hubbard Brook Experimental Forest. (3) The application of a simple but useful conceptual model for helping to frame questions and identify the ecological processes underlying observed changes or patterns in measured phenomena. (4) A rigorously developed and applied experimental design. (5) A carefully selected set of variables or entities to be measured.

As well as these five key design and implementation characteristics, successful programs also appear to have one or more of the following additional features (see also Strayer *et al.* 1986; Lovett *et al.* 2007): (1) Management relevance. (2) Strong and stable leadership. (3) Strong advocates. (4) Ongoing base funding. (5) Well-developed partnerships between important stakeholders. And, (6) Careful attention to database management and archiving of samples.

REFERENCES

Abal EG, Dennison WC and Bunn SE (2005) Setting. In *Heathy Waterways, Heathy Catchments: Making the Connection in South East Queensland.* (Eds EG Abal, SE Bunn and WC Dennison) pp. 13–34. Moreon Bay Catchments Partnership, Brisbane, Queensland.

Alberta Biodiversity Monitoring Institute (2009a) *Program overview.* Alberta Biodiversity Monitoring Institute, Edmonton http://www.alpac.ca/index.cfm?id=alberta_biodiversity

Alberta Biodiversity Monitoring Institute (2009b) The status of birds and vascular plants in Alberta's Lower Athabasca Planning Region. Preliminary Assessment. Alberta Biodiversity Monitoring Institute.

Alberta Biodiversity Monitoring Program (2005) Program overview and consultation backgrounder. ABMP Management Board.

Alberta Biodiversity Monitoring Program (2009) *Program overview and consultation backgrounder.* Alberta Biodiversity Monitoring Program, Edmonton, Canada http://www.alpac.ca/index.cfm?id=alberta_biodiversity

Beale R (2007) *If Trees Could Speak. Stories of Australia's Greatest Trees.* Allen and Unwin, Sydney.

Bormann FH and Likens GE (1967) Nutrient cycling. *Science* **155**, 424–429.

Bormann FH and Likens GE (1979) *Pattern and Process in a Forested Ecosystem.* Springer-Verlag, New York.

Bormann FH, Likens GE, Siccama TG, Pierce RS and Eaton JS (1974) The export of nutrients and recovery of stable conditions following deforestation at Hubbard Brook. *Ecological Monographs* **44**, 255–277.

Bormann FH, Siccama TG, Likens GE and Whittaker RH (1970) The Hubbard Brook Ecosystem Study: composition and dynamics of the tree stratum. *Ecological Monographs* **40**, 373–388.

Burton PJ, Messier C, Smith DW and Adamowicz WL (2003) *Towards Sustainable Management of the Boreal Forest.* National Research Council of Canada, Ottawa, Canada.

Buso DC, Likens GE and Eaton JS (2000) Chemistry of precipitation, stream water and lake water from the Hubbard Brook Ecosystem Study: A record of sampling protocols and analytical procedures. USDA Forest Service, Northeastern Research Station, Newtown Square, Pennsylvania.

Chilvers BL, Lawler IR, Macknight F, Marsh H, Noad M and Paterson R (2005) Moreton Bay, Queensland, Australia: an example of the co-existence of significant marine mammal populations and large-scale coastal development. *Biological Conservation* **122**, 559–571.

Cullen V (2005) *Down to the Sea for Science: 75 Years of Ocean Research, Education, and Exploration at the Woods Hole Oceanographic Institution.* Woods Hole Oceanographic Institution, Woods Hole, Massachusetts, USA.

Dennison WC and Abal EG (1999) Moreton Bay Study. South East Queensland Regional Water Quality Management Strategy, Brisbane.

Ecosystem Health Monitoring Program (2008) Report Card 2008 for the waterways and catchments of south-east Queensland. Ecosystem Health Monitoring Program, South East Queensland Healthy Waterways Partnership, Brisbane, Queensland.

Fahey TJ, Siccama TG, Driscoll CT, Likens GE, Campbell J, Johnson CE, Aber JD, Cole JJ, Fisk MC, Groffman PM, Holmes RT, Schwarz PA and Yanai RD (2005) The biogeochemistry of carbon at Hubbard Brook. *Biogeochemistry* **75**, 109–176.

Farr D, Lee P, Shank C and Stelfox B (1999) Conceptual framework and rationale for monitoring forest biodiversity in Alberta.

Fisher SG and Likens GE (1973) Energy flow in Bear Brook, New Hampshire: an integrative approach to stream ecosystem metabolism. *Ecological Monographs* **43**, 421–439.

Fox BJ (1982) Fire and mammalian secondary succession in an Australian coastal heath. *Ecology* **63**, 1332–1341.

Franklin JF, Lindenmayer DB, MacMahon JA, McKee A, Magnuson J, Perry DA, Waide R and Foster DR (2000) Threads of continuity: ecosystem disturbances, biological legacies and ecosystem recovery. *Conservation Biology in Practice* **1**, 8–16.

Gibbons P and Lindenmayer DB (2002) *Tree Hollows and Wildlife Conservation in Australia*. CSIRO Publishing, Melbourne.

Groffman PM, Driscoll CT, Eager C, Fisk MC, Fahey TJ, Holmes RT, Likens GE and Pardo L (2004a) A new governance structure for the Hubbard Brook Ecosystem Study. *Bulletin of the Ecological Society of America* **85**, 5–6.

Groffman PM, Driscoll CT, Likens GE, Fahey TJ, Holmes RT, Eagar C and Aber JD (2004b) Nor gloom of night: A new conceptual model for the Hubbard Brook Ecosystem Study. *BioScience* **54**, 139–148.

Groffman PM, Hardy JP, Driscoll CT and Fahey TJ (2006) Snow depth, soil freezing, and fluxes of carbon dioxide, nitrous oxide and methane in a northern hardwood forest. *Global Change Biology* **12**, 1748–1760.

Hero J-M, Castley JG, Malone M, Lawson and Magnusson WE (2009) Long-term ecological research in Australia: innovative approaches for future research. *Australian Zoologist*, (In press).

Holmes RT (2007) Understanding population change in migratory songbirds: long-term and experimental studies of Neotropical migrants in breeding and wintering areas. *Ibis (Suppl. 2)* **149**, 2–13.

Holmes RT, Sherry TW and Sturges FW (1986) Bird community dynamics in a temperate deciduous forest: long-term trends at Hubbard Brook. *Ecological Monographs* **56**, 201–220.

Hurlbert SH (1984) Pseudoreplication and the design of ecological field experiments. *Ecological Monographs* **54**, 187–211.

Keith H, Mackey B and Lindenmayer DB (2009) The world's most carbon-dense forests. *Proceedings of the National Academy of Sciences*, (In press).

Lamb EG, Bayne E, Holloway G, Schieck J, Soutin S, Herbers J and Haughland DL (2009) Indices for monitoring biodiversity change: are some more effective than others. *Ecological Indicators* **9**, 432–444.

Likens G and Buso D (2008) Long-term changes in streamwater chemistry following disturbance in the Hubbard Brook Experimental Forest, USA. *Verh Internat Verein Limnol* **30**, (In press).

Likens GE (Ed.) (1985a) *An Ecosystem Approach to Aquatic Ecology: Mirror Lake and its Environment*. Springer-Verlag, New York.

Likens GE (1992) *The Ecosystem Approach: Its Use and Abuse*. Ecology Institute, Oldendorf/Luhe, Germany.

Likens GE (2004) Some perspectives on long-term biogeochemical research from the Hubbard Brook Ecosystem Study. *Ecology* **85**, 2355–2362.

Likens GE and Bormann FH (1995) *Biogeochemistry of a Forested Ecoystem.* Second edition. Springer-Verlag, New York.

Likens GE, Bormann FH, Johnson NM, Fisher DW and Pierce RS (1970) Effects of forest cutting and herbicide treatment on nutrient budgets in the Hubbard Brook watershed-ecosystem. *Ecological Monographs* **40**, 23–47.

Likens GE, Bormann FH, Pierce RS, Eaton JS and Johnson NM (1977) *Biogeochemistry of a Forested Ecosystem.* Springer-Verlag, New York.

Likens GE, Driscoll CT, Buso DC, Mitchell MJ, Lovett GM, Bailey SW, Siccama TG, Reiners WA and Alewell C (2002) The biogeochemistry of sulfur at Hubbard Brook. *Biogeochemistry* **60**, 235–316.

Likens GE, Driscoll CT, Buso DC, Siccama TG, Johnson CE, Lovett GM, Fahey TJ, Reiners WA, Ryan DF, Martin CW and Bailey SW (1998) The biogeochemistry of calcium at Hubbard Brook. *Biogeochemistry* **41**, 89–173.

Likens GE, Driscoll CT, Buso DC, Siccama TG, Johnson CE, Ryan DF, Lovett GM, Fahey TJ and Reiners WA (1994) The biogeochemistry of potassium at Hubbard Brook. *Biogeochemistry* **25**, 61–125.

Likens GE and Franklin JF (2009) Ecosystem thinking in the Northern Forest – and beyond. *BioScience*, (In press).

Lindenmayer D and McCarthy MA (2002) Congruence between natural and human forest disturbance: a case study from Australian montane ash forests. *Forest Ecology and Management* **155**, 319–335.

Lindenmayer DB (2007) The Variable Harvest Retention System and its implications in the Mountain Ash forests of the Central Highlands of Victoria. Fenner School of Environment and Society, The Australian National University, Canberra.

Lindenmayer DB (2009) *Forest Pattern and Ecological Process: A Synthesis of 25 Years of Research.* CSIRO Publishing, Melbourne.

Lindenmayer DB and Burgman MA (2005) *Practical Conservation Biology.* CSIRO Publishing, Melbourne.

Lindenmayer DB, Craig SA, Linga T and Tanton MT (1991a) Public participation in stagwatching surveys for a rare mammal – applications for environmental education. *Australian Journal of Environmental Education* **7**, 63–70.

Lindenmayer DB and Cunningham RB (1997) Patterns of co-occurrence among arboreal marsupials in the forests of central Victoria, southeastern Australia. *Australian Journal of Ecology* **22**, 340–346.

Lindenmayer DB, Cunningham RB and Donnelly CF (1994) The conservation of arboreal marsupials in the montane ash forests of the Central Highlands of Victoria, south-eastern Australia. 6. The performance of statistical-models of the nest tree and habitat requirements of arboreal marsupials applied to new survey data. *Biological Conservation* **70**, 143–147.

Lindenmayer DB, Cunningham RB and Donnelly CF (1997) Decay and collapse of trees with hollows in eastern Australian forests – impacts on arboreal marsupials. *Ecological Applications* **7**, 625–641.

Lindenmayer DB, Cunningham RB, Donnelly CF and Franklin JF (2000) Structural features of old growth Australian montane ash forests. *Forest Ecology and Management* **134**, 189–204.

Lindenmayer DB, Cunningham RB, MacGregor C and Incoll RD (2003) A long-term monitoring study of the population dynamics of arboreal marsupials in the Central Highlands of Victoria. *Biological Conservation* **110**, 161–167.

Lindenmayer DB, Cunningham RB, Tanton MT, Nix HA and Smith AP (1991b) The conservation of arboreal marsupials in the montane ash forests of the Central Highlands of Victoria, south-east Australia. 3. The habitat requirements of Leadbeaters Possum Gymnobelideus-Leadbeateri and models of the diversity and abundance of arboreal marsupials. *Biological Conservation* **56**, 295–315.

Lindenmayer DB, Cunningham RB, Tanton MT and Smith AP (1990a) The conservation of arboreal marsupials in the montane ash forests of the Central Highlands of Victoria, south-east Australia. 2. The loss of trees with hollows and its implications for the conservation of Leadbeaters Possum Gymnobelideus-Leadbeateri Mccoy (Marsupialia, Petauridae). *Biological Conservation* **54**, 133–145.

Lindenmayer DB, Cunningham RB, Tanton MT, Smith AP and Nix HA (1990b) The conservation of arboreal marsupials in the montane ash forests of the Central Highlands of Victoria, south-east Australia.1. Factors influencing the occupancy of trees with hollows. *Biological Conservation* **54**, 111–131.

Lindenmayer DB, Cunningham RB, Tanton MT, Smith AP and Nix HA (1990c) The habitat requirements of the Mountain Brushtail Possum and the Greater Glider in the montane ash-type eucalypt forests of the Central Highlands of Victoria. *Australian Wildlife Research* **17**, 467–478.

Lindenmayer DB, Cunningham RB, Tanton MT, Smith AP and Nix HA (1991c) Characteristics of hollow-bearing trees occupied by arboreal marsupials in the montane ash forests of the Central Highlands of Victoria, south-east Australia. *Forest Ecology and Management* **40**, 289–308.

Lindenmayer DB and Franklin JF (2002) *Conserving Forest Biodiversity: A Comprehensive Multiscaled Approach.* Island Press, Washington.

Lindenmayer DB and Ough K (2006) Salvage harvesting in the montane ash forests of the Central Highlands of Victoria, south-eastern Australia. *Conservation Biology* **20**, 1005–1015.

Lindenmayer DB, Tanton MT and Norton TW (1990d) Leadbeater's Possum – a test case for integrated forestry. *Search* **21**, 156–159.

Lindenmayer DB, Welsh A, Donnelly CF and Meggs RA (1996) Use of nest trees By the Mountain Brushtail Possum (*Trichosurus Caninus*) (Phalangeridae, Marsupialia). 1. Number of occupied trees and frequency of tree use. *Wildlife Research* **23**, 343–361.

Lindenmayer DB and Wood J (2009) Long-term trend patterns in the decay, collapse and abundance of large trees in the wet ash forests of Victoria. *Canadian Journal of Forest Research*, (In review).

Lovett GM, Burns DA, Driscoll CT, Jenkins JC, Mitchell MJ, Rustad L, Shanley JB, Likens GE and Haeuber R (2007) Who needs environmental monitoring? *Frontiers in Ecology and the Environment* **5**, 253–260.

Lovett GM, Likens GE, Buso DC, Driscoll CT and Bailey SW (2005) The biogeochemistry of chlorine at Hubbard Brook, New Hampshire, USA. *Biogeochemistry* **72**, 191–232.

Mackey B, Lindenmayer DB, Gill AM, McCarthy MA and Lindesay JA (2002) *Wildlife, Fire and Future Climate: A Forest Ecosystem Analysis*. CSIRO Publishing, Melbourne.

Magnusson WE, Lima, AP, Luizao R, Costa FR, de Castillo CV and Kinupp VF (2005) RAPELD: a modfication of the Gentry method for biodiversity surveys in long-term ecological research sites. *Biota Neotropica* **5**, 1–6.

Marks PL (1974) The role of pin cherry (*Prunus pensylvanica* L.) in the maintenance of stability in northern hardwood ecosystems. *Ecological Monographs* **44**, 73–88.

McDonald M, Blair R, Bolgrien D, Brown B, Dlugosz J, Hale S, Hedtke S, Heggem D, Jackson L, Jones K, Levinson B, Linthurst R, Messer J, Olsen A, Paul J, Paulsen S, Stoddard J, Summers K and Veith G (2004) The U.S. Environmental Protection Agency's Environmental Monitoring and Assessment Program. In *Environmental Monitoring*. (Ed. GB Wiersma). CRC Press.

Messer JJ, Linthurst RA and Overton WS (1991) An EPA program for monitoring ecological status and trends. *Environmental Monitoring and Assessment* **17**, 67–78.

Moreton Bay Waterways and Catchments Partnership (2003) Annual Report 2002–2003. Moreton Bay Waterways and Catchments Partnership, Brisbane.

Moreton Bay Waterways and Catchments Partnership (2004) Report Card 2004 for the waterways of south east Queensland. Moreton Bay Waterways and Catchments Partnership, Brisbane.

O'Neill G (2008) Jump-starting environmental monitoring. *Ecos* **143**, 14–17.

Parr CL and Andersen AN (2006) Patch mosaic burning for biodiversity conservation: a critique of the pyrodiversity paradigm. *Conservation Biology* **20**, 1610–1619.

Reilly WK (1989) Measuring for environmental results. *EPA Journal* **25**, 2–4.

Rothamsted Research (2006) Guide to classical and other long-term experiments, datasets and sample archive. Lawes Agricultural Trust, Bury St. Edmunds, England.

Rothamsted Research (2009) Making a difference: the past and future economic and societal impact of Rothamsted Research. Rothamsted Research, Harpenden, England.

Salsburg D (2001) *The Lady Tasting Tea. How Statistics Revolutionized Science in the Twentieth Century.* WH Freeman, New York.

Shank C, Schieck J and Farr D (2002) The Alberta Biodiversity Monitoring Program: Updated Technical Summary. Alberta Biodiversity Monitoring Program.

Shiel D and Burslem FR (2003) Disturbing hypotheses in tropical forests. *Trends in Ecology and Evolution* **18**, 18–26.

Siccama, TG, Fahey, TJ, Johnson, CE, Sherry, TW, Denny, EG, Girdler, EB, Likens, GE and Schwartz, PA (2007) Population and biomass dynamics of trees in a northern hardwood forest at Hubbard Brook. *Canadian Journal of Forest Research* **37**, 737–749.

Skinner JL, Gilliam E and Rohlin C-J (1998) The demographic future of the Moreton region. In *Moreton Bay and catchment.* (Eds R Tibbetts, N Hall and WC Dennison) pp. 245–265. School of Marine Science, University of Queensland.

Smith AP and Lindenmayer D (1988) Tree Hollow Requirements of Leadbeaters Possum and Other Possums and Gliders in Timber Production Ash Forests of the Victorian Central Highlands. *Australian Wildlife Research* **15**, 347–362.

South East Queensland Healthy Waterways Partnership (2007) South East Queensland Healthy Waterways Strategy 2007–2012. Ecosystem health monitoring program action plan. South East Queensland Healthy Partnership

State of the Environment Advisory Council (1996) State of the Environment Australia 1996. Report for Commonwealth Minister for the Environment. CSIRO, Melbourne.

State of the Environment Report (2001) Biodiversity. Commonwealth of Australia, Canberra.

Stevens DL (1994) Implementation of a national monitoring program. *Journal of Environmental Management* **42**, 1–29.

Strayer DL, Glitzenstein JS, Jones C, Kolasa J, Likens GE, McDonnell M, Parker GG and Pickett STA (1986) Long-term ecological studies: an illustrated account of their design, operation, and importance to ecology. Institute of Ecosystem Studies, Millbrook, New York.

The Heinz Center (2008) The State of the Nation's Ecosystems 2008. The H. John Heinz III Center for Science, Economics and the Environment and Island Press, Washington, D.C.

Tilman GD (2003) *NEON: Addressing the Nation's Environmental Challenges.* National Academy Press, Washington, D.C.

Van Horne B and Wiens J.A. (1991) Forest bird habitat suitability models and the development of general habitat models. U.S. Fish and Wildlife Service, Washington, D.C.

Whelan RJ (1995) *The Ecology of Fire*. Cambridge University Press, Cambridge.

Whittaker RH, Bormann FH, Likens GE and Siccama TG (1974) The Hubbard Brook Ecosystem Study: forest biomass and production. *Ecological Monographs* **44**, 233–254.

Winter TC and Likens GE (Eds) (2009) *Mirror Lake: interactions among air, land and water*. University of California Press, Los Angeles.

Wright-Stow AE and Winterbourn MJ (2003) How well do New Zealand's stream-monitoring indicators, the Macroinvertebrate Community Index and its quantative variant, correspond? *New Zealand Journal of Marine and Freshwater Research* **37**, 461–470.

Chapter 5

The upshot – our general conclusions

Long-term ecological monitoring programs are fundamental to evidence-based environmental decision-making. They are essential to gauge the effectiveness of management interventions (Krebs 1991; Field *et al.* 2007). They will become increasingly critical as part of efforts to mitigate against, or better adapt to, the effects of rapid climate change and human-accelerated environmental change (Likens 1991; Lovett *et al.* 2007; Steffen *et al.* 2009). It is now perhaps more important than ever to ensure that the currently limited resources expended on environmental management in general and long-term research and monitoring in particular are spent as effectively as possible. As we argued at the start of this book, we believe that many of the attributes are generic and apply equally to biodiversity monitoring as they do to environmental monitoring and are as relevant to marine ecosystems as they are to terrestrial and inland aquatic ecosystems.

This book has outlined some of the attributes that we consider to be pivotal for effective long-term ecological monitoring programs. We are fully cognisant of the fact that there is no such thing as a perfect monitoring program. The deficiencies in our own work (see Chapter 4) bear testament to this. However, it is clear that we must improve on the very poor record of ecological monitoring to date. We must make it more efficient, more effective and more successful. Only then will governments, private foundations and the general public be willing to support the significant increases in funding urgently needed for environmental monitoring. The Adaptive Monitoring paradigm we present is a logical framework for drawing together many of the attributes needed to improve all kinds of monitoring, but particularly mandated monitoring and question-driven monitoring programs (see Chapter 3).

CHANGES IN CULTURE NEEDED TO FACILITATE MONITORING

As important as we believe that our Adaptive Monitoring framework is, many other factors outside this framework conspire to prevent monitoring programs from being successful and new ones from being instigated. They also conspire to make many monitoring programs ineffective. We outline these in the following section, and argue that the culture of science and indeed many aspects of society *per se*, mitigate strongly against monitoring programs being established and maintained. We believe these problems must be tackled if improvements in the understanding of the array of environmental problems facing humanity are to be achieved.

The academic culture and rewards systems

We are acutely aware that some researchers do not have the right psyche to conduct long-term monitoring programs, for instance, because they get bored or because long-term studies have opportunity costs that preclude researchers from doing other things. Also, there is a deeply ingrained scientific culture and associated reward system which creates substantial disincentives to undertake long-term ecological monitoring.

First, there is a widespread and increasing emphasis on 'newsy', short or provocative articles in scientific journals (e.g. through page-length and citation constraints). This emphasis favours multiple, brief publications over longer works of ecological synthesis. It penalises long-term studies, which are often best reported as major bodies of work drawing together many parallel themes of research. Long-term monitoring programs are also difficult for scientists in the early stages of their careers because they may not generate publications rapidly enough for them to build a track record of publications for promotion or other rewards.

Second, there is a current emphasis from editors to reduce the number of citations in scholarly papers, presumably to save journal space. This limitation, combined with some journals now 'requiring' citations from the journal where the paper is being published to increase the journal's impact factor (Silver 2006), produces both a real and an ethical dilemma for scientists attempting to synthesise a large body of information based on long-term monitoring. It is interesting to note, however, that of the journals of the American Ecological Society, *Ecological Monographs* which produces long, data-rich articles has a higher citation impact factor (8.1) than does its stablemate *Ecology* (4.8) in which shorter papers are produced (based on the Thompson Scientific Journal Citation Reports, February 2009).

Third, the bibliometric emphasis in academic reward systems directs scientists to produce many short articles rather than fewer (longer) synthesis publications (the 'LPU' or Least Publishable Unit issue, see Likens 1998). This emphasis has led to an information 'superglut', which no one can read fully or carefully. It also has meant that people are not reading the literature or are overlooking important earlier scientific articles (Belovsky *et al.* 2004), 're-inventing wheels' and purporting to be making discoveries when they are actually making re-discoveries. Even powerful searchable literature databases such as the Web of Science are limited in how far back in time they can go and they do not allow for scientific articles to be located when relevant results are not apparent from the title, abstract or key words.

Fourth, scientific culture favours discoveries and new work rather than maintaining ongoing work. This emphasis is a disincentive for young, upcoming scientists to take over pre-existing projects and provide continuity in leadership for long-term projects.

Fifth, there is an emphasis on short-term funding: grants and projects are typically for three years or less. However, it is surprising to us how many papers in the literature regard two to three years of study as long-term monitoring (e.g. Pavlik and Barbour 1988; Buck *et al.* 1996; Goldstein and Beyer 1999). Conversely, flat-funding on multiple-year grants is a prognosis for future failure, as most of the cost in long-term projects is for salaries.

Sixth, ecology has long been plagued by fads and ill-conceived or poorly defined concepts. This approach doesn't help promote a culture of careful, question-setting or foster a psyche of making prolonged sets of repeated measurements. Moreover, a culture has developed in recent years to teach and research what is profitable, not necessarily what is important.

Seventh, many aspects of ecology also have been dominated by a spatial bias with much less emphasis on temporal effects. When temporal factors have been explored they often have been examined using space-for-time substitution, rather than true time-series data.

Eighth, there often has been a focus on modelling *per se* rather than empirical data collection and analysis, even though models need to be based on empirical data, and are tools and not an end point in themselves (Burgman *et al.* 1993; Canham *et al.* 2003). There also has been a rapid increase in the amount of 'content-free' simulation modelling almost devoid of any empirical data. While this kind of modelling is an understandable approach because modelling is comparatively cheap, can generate results quickly, and leads to numerous papers, we caution that virtual reality can quickly descend into real stupidity (or fantasy).

Ninth, scientists are increasingly pushed to work simultaneously across many different projects and many different disciplines, i.e. multi-tasking (Forgasz and Leder 2006). We are chronic multi-taskers and don't deny that many multi-taskers can be very productive, but many people currently are badly overcommitted (including ourselves). Multi-tasking can be quite distracting to most scientists, by prohibiting them from thinking deeply. Relative to the topic of this book, we believe that the multi-tasking culture is placing an emphasis on quantity rather than quality. The multi-tasking approach to science can lead to fragmentation of ideas, of funding, and of time (with a focus on deadlines). We understand that multi-tasking is a part of modern life, but we hope that the modern academic culture will provide the opportunity for young scientists to focus on some long-term projects.

Tenth, many senior scientists do not get to spend time in the field and view first-hand and over time, the environmental changes that they are interested in and/or are working on.

Eleventh, many universities have moved away from field courses. They are expensive to run and they can be hindered by occupational, health and safety issues as well as liability risks. Several field and remote research stations have been closed, are close to closing or dramatically altered in recent decades (Hildrew 2004). These changes contribute to a loss of natural history skills as well as natural history information (Noss 1996) and a lack of training in how to do the empirical component of long-term monitoring. This loss will, in turn, lead to limited future cohorts of young researchers attracted to long-term ecological monitoring programs.

Finally, career development in science often promotes moving between institutions. There is some value in such moves, such as preventing 'inbreeding depression' resulting from a person spending their entire career at the one place. It is also often the only way for scientists to gain promotion and increases in salary. However, we consider that frequent shifts between institutions make it more difficult to maintain continuity at a given site/location over a prolonged period.

We strongly believe that the culture of science needs careful re-examination to tackle head-on many of the problems we have touched on here. Some of these developing cultural practices warrant changing in ways that do not continue to penalise severely any scientific engagement in long-term monitoring. In the specific case of long-term monitoring programs, there will be considerable value in ensuring that a thorough search of past literature is completed before new studies are initiated (Green and Balmford 2005). We also believe there may be value in young academics being encouraged to establish long-term programs if they are fortunate enough to secure a permanent (tenured) position. It is possible to initiate a monitoring program prior to tenure but we fully understand that this has substantial risks in the academic world.

Structure of organisations

The structure of many organisations is far from conducive for instigating and then maintaining long-term monitoring programs. Many organisations have high staff turnover and are characterised by a rapid loss of corporate culture. There is limited or no psyche of long-term studies (O'Neill 2008) or things allied with them like fastidious data and sample curation or long-term data management. In addition, there is usually an emphasis on reducing staff numbers in these organisations during budget crises, leading to a severe drop in morale. Yet, people on the ground are essential for successful monitoring.

Many organisations involved in environmental management have focused on the procurement of equipment rather than on retaining staff. However, as we discuss in Chapter 2, a focus on built infrastructure can create substantial problems such as breaching the integrity of time series data, precluding studies that are guided by a robust experimental design, and creating problems for data analysis by generating vast datasets (see Berkelmans and Hendee 2002).

Part of the recent focus on built infrastructure in these organisations concerns the development of equipment to gather and transmit real-time data. An example is remotely stationed flux towers or temperature sensors that collect and transmit information at rapid intervals. We believe these approaches can have inherent value but that field measurements are vital to calibrate these instruments and to identify when these instruments produce incorrect or misleading information. Moreover, such kinds of instrumentation may create a disincentive for people to go into the field and better understand how an ecosystem is functioning. Finally, a robust design built on questions needs to drive this type of data collection to avoid being overwhelmed by masses of unwanted or unneeded data.

Many organisations contract out major projects (outsourcing), for example, to consulting companies. Other organisations like the CSIRO in Australia are moving away from on-ground work. The business plan of these organisations means they are no longer capable of doing truly long-term monitoring because they are required to do other kinds of work such as consulting or short-term contracts. Moreover, many mandated monitoring programs change with the politics of the day, which can lead to termination of ongoing programs and false starts in others.

Many scientists and resource managers are on short-term, non-continuing contracts. Such a lack of certainty makes it unlikely that they will want to set up long-term monitoring programs.

The points we make above suggest to us that current organisational mandates, structures and cultures are often far from conducive to establishing and maintaining long-term monitoring programs. We believe that this culture must be changed in at least some organisations (Caughlan and Oakley 2001).

Intellectual property issues

Successful long-term research and monitoring programs result in the collection of high-quality empirical data and are characterised by high-quality data management. However, an important, but often unresolved issue is intellectual property and data sharing in the wider ecological and resource management communities. Only rarely have reasonable and ethical rules of engagement been developed for data sharing between those who gather long-term field data and others who desire access to those data for modelling, data mining and other analyses. Without appropriate attention to intellectual property issues at the beginning of a study, the development of better ways of data sharing (e.g. Jones *et al.* 2006) will be impaired and the full potential of valuable empirical data for enhanced environmental management will not be realised (Bertzky and Stoll-Kleemann 2008). A policy regarding public data dissemination should be thought through and stated early in the process of setting up a study. Likewise, within teams of scientists doing long-term research and monitoring, there needs to be a clear, articulated understanding, also at the beginning of the effort, about the role of team members and the use and attribution of data collected by individuals in the team (Likens 2001).

Funding

Access to funding is an obvious factor influencing the success of monitoring programs. Many aspects of funding are not well suited to the establishment and maintenance of such programs. Monitoring programs are often seen as a luxury and not a core part of the focus of many resource management organisations. They are therefore usually the last initiatives to be funded (after all other, higher priority ones have been supported) and the first ones to be cut during budget shortfalls. In addition, budget cycles emphasise short-term projects with rapid achievement of milestones. Funding initiatives of one to three years are rarely congruent with the time frames appropriate for effective monitoring. Thus, there often is a fundamental mismatch between long-term environmental management aspirations and short-term financial realities.

A limited number of monitoring programs now operate through the support of long-term endowments. Our case study in Chapter 4 on the 175-year research program at Rothamsted in England provides one of the best known examples worldwide. Although such long-term funding is a welcome relief from the constant tribulation of maintaining the funding for a long-term project, we acknowledge that this approach needs to be applied carefully to ensure that guaranteed long-term funding does not create disincentives to be productive, innovative, and to add exciting new projects that contribute additional insights to an overall body of work – a little 'hunger' can be a good thing! Too much hunger is not.

Societal culture

Many of the traits needed to guide monitoring programs – endurance, tenacity, persistence, thoroughness – are not particularly common ones in western society. Rather, society has developed characteristics which are the antithesis of these:

- An epidemic of busyness (Likens 1998) created by cell phones, email and other rapid communication technology and ease of travel to meetings worldwide. While these innovations can assist the scientific enterprise in many ways, this epidemic can restrict time for clear thinking, thoroughness and creativity, which are essential to frame incisive ecological questions and conduct effective monitoring.
- Nature Deficit Disorder or a disconnect between people in modern society and their natural environment (Louv 2005; Zaradic and Pergams 2007; Pergams and Zaradic 2008). This disconnect is allied with a loss of the natural history skills in the general community (Noss 1996) that are essential for good monitoring and long-term research (see Box 5.3).
- Politicisation of administrative decisions.
- Rapid turnover in employment.

In summary, it appears to us that a perverse outcome of the culture of western society, and parts of it like science culture and its reward system, is that this culture has inadvertently created disincentives to

---

BOX 5.1 'CLOSE SHAVES'

Close shaves in maintaining long-term research and monitoring programs are common. Charles David Keeling had several where his CO_2 monitoring program at Mauna Loa (see Box 3.4 in Chapter 3) came very close to being terminated. Apparently, Keeling had a reputation for being 'grumpy'. We can easily relate to that as it is very difficult and stressful to keep monitoring funded and operational, especially if there is a strong belief that data gaps are a major nemesis. Similar, 'close shaves' have occurred on more than one occasion in the Hubbard Brook Ecosystem Study and in the Victorian Central Highlands Study, including as recently as mid-2009. Again, this problem is not uncommon and the challenge is to be nimble enough and innovative enough in finding ways to meet these threats to the integrity of the long-term records being maintained. With hindsight, it is now clear how important it was that the 'Keeling curve' not be terminated.

---

develop the monitoring systems to improve the management of ecosystems on which humankind depends. We are unsure how to best tackle major deep-seated issues like the culture of western and scientific cultures. Some corporations and other organisations have attempted to tackle problems associated with issues such as the epidemic of busyness through small steps like imposing email-free days. Far more substantial changes are required. Those with quite different skills from ours (e.g. Louv 2005), such as in psychology, sociology, public and science policy, and institutional arrangements, need to examine these problems and suggest ways to try to rectify them.

GOOD THINGS THAT CAN COME FROM NON-QUESTION-BASED MONITORING

We have spent much of this book highlighting what we believe constitutes ineffective monitoring. We also have outlined an Adaptive Monitoring approach (Lindenmayer and Likens 2009) to gather many of the features of effective monitoring programs within a single coherent and logical framework. However, there are examples where long-term studies have produced valuable information, even when they have not been guided by carefully crafted scientific questions, no formal conceptual model was used to identify those questions, and there was a noticeable absence of a statistical-based experimental design. We highlight in Box 5.3 two outstanding examples of studies of this kind and we include them here to illustrate that

---

BOX. 5.2 LEADERSHIP SUCCESSION

Planning for leadership succession is very important in the maintenance of long-term monitoring programs (see Chapter 2). However, it is very difficult to do (and neither of us have done it well!). There are many reasons, including: **(1)** difficulty in putting out the 'fire in the belly' to keep a successful project running; **(2)** ego investment on the part of the chief investigator; **(3)** not admitting that succession is needed (at least not now); and **(4)** intellectual property issues.

Issues of leadership succession need far closer attention to ensure the value of monitoring programs does not die along with their instigators. For example, to the best of our knowledge, few if any universities or research institutes would make an academic appointment to maintain an already established long-term ecological research or monitoring program. Thus, the problems of a lack of culture in succession planning in universities and research institutes may well warrant re-examination.

---

we are not zealots in pushing our Adaptive Monitoring framework to the total exclusion of all other approaches.

We readily acknowledge that many different approaches and perspectives are important in the evolution of improved long-term ecological research and monitoring programs. We do, however, note that both case studies summarised in Box 5.3 are characterised by three features which are also common to effective monitoring programs (see Chapter 3): **(1)** they were maintained by a competent, dedicated and highly motivated individual; **(2)** record keeping was accurate and immaculate; and **(3)** they were driven by curiosity.

THE NEXT BIG CHALLENGE – INTEGRATING DIFFERENT KINDS OF MONITORING

The material we have presented throughout this book, together with the series of case studies in Chapter 4, clearly show that there are several kinds of long-term monitoring programs. For the general purposes of this book, we have crudely assigned them into three broad categories: question-driven monitoring, mandated monitoring and curiosity-driven or passive monitoring. Different kinds of studies within these broad categories are conducted in different ways and at different scales. This diversity is fundamental to our Adaptive Monitoring framework, which is clearly **not** a one-size-fits-all approach, but rather emphasises a need to focus on well-crafted questions resulting in a study design, set of attributes and an

BOX 5.3 WHEN GOOD THINGS COME FROM A LACK OF FORMAL, TESTABLE, SCIENTIFICALLY DRIVEN QUESTIONS ...

Because of an intense desire to know more about the natural world and coupled with a strong discipline of recording natural history information in a personal journal, Aldo Leopold accumulated long-term (13 years) data on weather patterns and phenological records of migratory bird arrivals and departures, plant flowering times, etc. for central Wisconsin, USA. After his death in 1948, these long-term observations were restarted by his daughter Nina and her husband Charles Bradley in 1976 and have been continued to the present. This rich record of natural history observations has provided significant insights into the effects of climate change on the timing of biological phenomena for this area (Bradley *et al.* 1999), and is available to researchers at the Aldo Leopold Legacy Center in Baraboo, Wisconsin and worldwide (www.aldoleopold.org) .

Similarly, Daniel Smiley religiously recorded weather and a broad range of natural history events for more than 60 years at his family's property in the New Paltz area of the Shawangunk Mountains of New York State, USA. These data were collected carefully, but stored mostly on index cards in cardboard boxes. Because this information was potentially so important, one of us (GEL) strongly urged Mr Smiley in the late 1970s to organise these cards and collections and store them in a fire-proof facility. This suggestion was supported by others and currently this collection of data is computerised, secure and available to researchers as part of the Daniel Smiley Research Center at the Mohonk Preserve and worldwide (www.mohonkpreserve.org). Several peer-reviewed publications have utilised these daily observations of phenology, rainfall amount, air temperature, ice in/ice out data for a small lake on the property, and acidity of surface waters (Cook *et al.* 2008).

Both of these extraordinary men have died, but their legacy lives on, and the long-term records they maintained are being continued by others. These two didn't have a formal conceptual model (although they undoubtedly had a mental one), a statistical design for the activity, or formal question(s) (but they had ample curiosity) to guide these data collections. Yet it is clear that the rigor and tenacity of doing careful, long-term measurements paid off in providing important insights about how nature works and can change over time.

implementation approach that will be different in each monitoring program (see Chapter 3).

Yet, politicians and high-level policy-makers will want some kind of world-, state- or national-level reflection of environmental performance. A large and growing number of regional, state/provincial, national and

Figure 5.1 A. Aldo Leopold (courtesy of the Aldo Leopold Foundation). B. Daniel Smiley (right). (Photo by Gerd Ludwig (1986) courtesy of Mohonk Preserve Daniel Smiley Research Center)

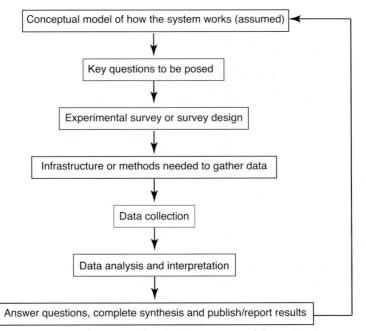

Figure 5.2 Sequence of steps underpinning a successful monitoring program.

international organisations are producing 'state of the environment' reports (see www.cnie.org for a good, but partial listing of the sources for these reports). Examples include the highly visible, Worldwatch Institute's annual State of the World reports; The State of The Nation's Ecosystems for the USA (The Heinz Center 2008), The Council on Environmental Quality (CEQ) produced annual reports from 1970 until 1997 and then sporadically. In 2000 the CEQ produced the 2000 Report to the President of the USA (Council 1996; State of the Environment Report 2001; Bastin 2008). Countless United Nations documents on the state of the planet's natural resources and its environment are produced (e.g. United Nations Environment Program (UNEP) 1999; Food and Agriculture Organisation of the United Nations 2007).

These mandated monitoring programs will often produce coarse-level summaries of temporal changes in resource condition (e.g. 'status reports'), but provide limited understanding about the site-specific mechanisms that have given rise to those changes. The large spatial scale of this information also may not be particularly useful for guiding targeted on-the-ground management interventions to improve environmental conditions in a given location.

Conversely, question-driven, long-term monitoring programs will often be operating at the level of sites, landscapes or regions. When they are based on well-defined and scientifically tested questions (as well as many other features), they can provide important long-term environmental data on emerging environmental problems, as well as insights about the mechanisms or ecological processes giving rise to these emergent patterns. Such programs, in turn, can be valuable for informing resource management. However, spatial generalisation from question-driven, long-term monitoring programs is difficult because the results from such studies may not extrapolate well to other regions, states or to the national level. That is, it is not straightforward to produce national perspectives on environmental conditions by integrating across such kinds of different site-level, landscape-level, or region-level studies. Thus, these kinds of detailed programs are usually one-of-a-kind projects that do not produce data at the scale many governments want or need. For example, even if it were possible to roll out the excellent 'report card' system for Moreton Bay in south-east Queensland, Australia (see Chapter 4) to the rest of Australia's many estuaries, we are not aware of a scientifically defensible method that would enable a single, nationally aggregated estuary assessment.

Therefore, there is an inherent tension between state- and national-level mandated monitoring and site- and region-based monitoring as well as between academic- and organisation-based monitoring programs. This tension occurs because these are often quite disparate programs. For example, we were stunned to note that no data from the 26 Long-Term Ecological Research (LTER) sites costing US taxpayers ~$23 million per year were explicitly included in the USA's State of the Nation's Ecosystems report (The Heinz Center 2008).

The tension between mandated monitoring programs and site- and region-based monitoring programs is reminiscent of tensions between top-down and bottom-up approaches in ecological thinking and research approaches. As in the case of taking advantage of the different methods of study in ecology to facilitate progress, there also must be ways to capitalise on synergies between national- and state-based mandated monitoring and question-driven monitoring.

Many authors have argued that ecology is a case-study discipline (e.g. Shrader-Frechette and McCoy 1993) and it is clear that as outstanding as some particular long-term programs have been, such as those at Rothamsted (England) or the Experimental Lakes Area in Ontario (Canada), they are one-offs that are virtually impossible to replicate elsewhere. However, we believe that these kinds of projects serve as 'in depth, reference models' often identifying major environmental problems (e.g. atmospheric CO_2 increase at Mauna Loa, acid rain at the Hubbard Brook Experimental Forest) and showing what key environmental changes or important ecological processes are occurring in other places. These kinds of long-term research and monitoring programs have led to major discoveries and resulted in very large problems in ecology and environmental management being identified and/or addressed. For example, while it is very difficult to extend the results of the Hubbard Brook Ecosystem Study beyond the Hubbard Brook Valley, the findings from the long-term research and monitoring at the Hubbard Brook Experimental Forest clearly suggested that acid rain and its effects were far more extensive throughout North America. The long-term data from the Hubbard Brook Ecosystem Study underpinned the passage of the 1990 Clean Air Act Amendments in the USA, primarily because the results were so long and of such unassailable quality (see Chapter 4). Moreover, the research of the Hubbard Brook Ecosystem Study in New Hampshire and the Experimental Lakes Area in Ontario helped to catalyse the commencement of national networks for precipitation chemistry in the USA and Canada (many other federal programs and individuals, including James Galloway and Ellis Cowling, were instrumental as well). The important lesson then is that leaders of site-based monitoring programs should think about the broader (regional, state, province or national) implications of their findings and discoveries, including the implications of site-based work as models for larger-scaled, mandated monitoring programs.

We also believe that the fundamental characteristics of some of the best examples of question-driven monitoring programs (well-defined questions, well-articulated conceptual models, rigorous experimental designs) are features that should be much more widely embraced as part of efforts to improve mandated monitoring programs. Hence, the Adaptive Monitoring framework we describe in Chapter 3 and the iterative steps that comprise the framework (Figure 5.2), are just as relevant to mandated monitoring programs as they are to question-driven monitoring programs. We argue that any kind of monitoring program will be effective only when it is based on well-defined questions, makes use of a well formulated conceptual model, and is guided by a carefully crafted experimental design. This formula may sound trite, but in the process of writing this book, we have been shocked at how often these seemingly simple ingredients are missing from a very large number of monitoring programs. For example, we suggest that programs like the US-LTER network, NEON, ABMP and TERN could be re-examined against the core principles of our Adaptive

Monitoring framework with a goal of making them more effective, more successful and able to garner greater public support.

The simultaneous devastating fires in Victoria and floods in Queensland and the Northern Territory of Australia during the summer of 2008–2009 starkly emphasise the critical need for properly designed and adequately funded monitoring programs in that country. The social costs of these disasters in terms of loss of human life and property were horrific. At the same time, the change and degradation of natural ecosystems in these areas were enormous, yet they could not be measured quantitatively because of an inadequate monitoring network (Lindenmayer *et al.* 2009). Therefore, critical and urgent management decisions needed to protect water supplies, soils, wildlife, and regenerating forests had to be based on limited information rather than strong ecological understanding and knowledge. The USA's National Science Foundation has had a small program for immediate response and funding following such disasters (Special Grants for Ecological Research). This program has been very important because of its responsive nature following major disasters. We would argue that all countries should be prepared in this way to develop key ecological information via research and monitoring to guide managers following major natural disturbances (Lindenmayer *et al.* 2009).

APPROACHES TO INTEGRATE DATA FROM QUESTION-DRIVEN MONITORING AND MANDATED MONITORING

There are advantages and disadvantages of question-led monitoring and large-scale mandated monitoring. The challenge is to find ways to integrate data and insights from them in ways that are useful for environmental management. To meet this challenge we need to overcome some impediments.

First, attempts to coordinate across programs would require a uniform set of protocols to facilitate data compatibility. This is a 'one-size-fits-all' approach and we outlined the suite of problems generic monitoring frameworks can create in Chapter 2. In fact, enforcing the measurement of a common string of variables across sites could result in a 'race to the bottom'. That is, it may lead to a very crude set of common measurements of limited value for environmental management. Many measurements in, for example, long-leaf pine ecosystems in south-eastern USA, which are strongly fire-dependent, may be irrelevant to the deserts of Antarctica or tropical rainforests of Puerto Rico.

Second, it remains unclear how to combine sensibly the metrics for environmental conditions that have been estimated or calculated in different systems. There is a long, but largely unsuccessful, history of this kind of problem in other topics in ecology. Examples include the difficulties of combining sub-indices for habitat attributes in constructing Habitat Suitability Index models (reviewed by Van Horne and Wiens 1991; Lindenmayer and Burgman 2005) and combining landscape indices into meaningful measures of landscape cover (Cale and Hobbs 1994; McAlpine *et al.* 2002). It seems to us that combining outcomes from quite different monitoring programs is a broadly similar kind of problem, albeit at large spatial scales and over longer time frames. As an example, poor environmental performance in one place added to a good performance in another could be combined to provide an average overall result and to suggest that the environmental conditions are reasonable, but this result would obscure the fact that environmental conditions are degrading in some places. In Australia there are proposals to create a set of National Environment Accounts, similar to those which are used to gauge economic trends (e.g. Gross Domestic Product, employment numbers, budget surpluses and budget deficits) (Wentworth Group 2008). Such accounts would need to be built on high-quality environmental datasets and combine information from a range of sources to facilitate the calculation of credible metrics of environmental condition (Wentworth Group 2008). There have been recent attempts to develop approaches to measure environmental performance better (Nielsen *et al.* 2007; McDonald *et al.* 2008; Lamb *et al.* 2009). These are promising. However, they are still in their infancy and in many cases often their focus is relatively narrow (e.g. on the amount of area protected).

A third impediment that needs to be overcome is making long-term data readily accessible to the scientific community and others. At the same time the problems of protecting intellectual property through attribution must be resolved clearly and early in the establishment of a monitoring program.

We believe that many of the arguments in the scientific and resource management literatures about monitoring frameworks and frustrations about failed monitoring programs stem from a failure to recognise the inherent values of, and differences between, large-scale mandated monitoring programs and smaller-scaled question-driven monitoring programs. We believe the next major challenge for long-term monitoring is to work out how to combine the datasets, results and outcomes that are conducted at different scales and in different ways to produce integrated assessments useful to decision-makers. There may well be methods that have been used to develop broadly based state-, province- or national-level economic indicators as well as track economic performance in different (often more localised) sectors of economies, which may be usefully applied in solving problems of aggregating datasets from environmental monitoring programs. The development of such approaches could help reflect environmental conditions at local scales as well as highlight overall environmental performance at larger (aggregated scales) (e.g. at a state, province or national level). However, we readily admit that we currently do not know how to do this for environmental monitoring programs and associated datasets in ways that are scientifically defensible, of value for resource managers and useful to policy-makers. We know that many readers will find our admission of ignorance to be unsatisfactory and frustrating. However, unless this challenge is resolved, our ability to deal with pressing problems such as rapid climate change and human-accelerated environmental change will be severely limited. Overcoming this challenge should be a primary topic for further published discussions and a focused conference that builds on the insights summarised in this volume.

REFERENCES

Bastin G (2008) Rangelands 2008 – taking the pulse. Commonwealth of Australia, Canberra.

Belovsky GE, Botkin DB, Crowl TA, Cummins KW, Franklin JF, Hunter ML, Joern A, Lindenmayer DB, MacMahon JA, Margules CR and Scott JM (2004) Ten suggestions to strengthen the science of ecology. *Bioscience* **54**, 345–351.

Berkelmans R and Hendee JC (2002) Automatic weather stations: tools for managing and monitoring potential impacts to coral reefs. *Marine Technology Society Journal* **36**, 29–38.

Bertzky M and Stoll-Kleemann S (2008) Multi-level discrepancies with sharing data on protected areas: What we have and what we need for the global village. *Journal of Environmental Management*, (In press).

Bradley N, Leopold AC, Ross J and Huffaker W (1999) Phenological changes reflect climate change in Wisconsin. *Proceedings of the National Academy of Sciences* **96**, 9701–9704.

Buck JA, Brewer LW, Hooper MJ, Cobb GP and Kendall RJ (1996) Monitoring Great Horned Owls for pesticide exposure in southcentral Iowa. *Journal of Wildlife Management* **60**, 321–331.

Burgman MA, Ferson S and Akçakaya HR (1993) *Risk Assessment in Conservation Biology*. Chapman and Hall, New York, London.

Cale PG and Hobbs RJ (1994) Landscape heterogeneity indices: problems of scale and applicability, with particular reference to animal habitat description. *Pacific Conservation Biology* **1**, 183–193.

Canham CD, Cole JJ and Lauenroth WK (Eds) (2003) *Models in Ecosystem Science*. Princeton University Press, Princeton, New Jersey.

Caughlan L and Oakley KL (2001) Cost considerations for long-term ecological monitoring. *Ecological Indicators* **1**, 123–134.

Cook BI, Cook ER, Huth PC, Thompson JE, Forster A and Smiley D (2008) A cross-taxa phenological dataset from Mohonk Lake, NY and its relationship to climate. *International Journal of Climatology* **28**, 1369–1383.

Council SotEA (1996) State of the Environment Australia 1996. Report for Commonwealth Minister for the Environment. CSIRO, Melbourne.

Field SA, O'Connor PJ, Tyre AJ and Possingham HP (2007) Making monitoring meaningful. *Austral Ecology* **32**, 485–491.

Food and Agriculture Organisation of the United Nations (2007) State of the world's forests. Food and Agriculture Organisation of the United Nations, Rome, Italy.

Forgasz HJ and Leder GC (2006) Academic life: monitoring work patterns and daily activities. *The Australian Educational Researcher* **33**, 1–22.

Goldstein A and Beyer J (1999) Monitoring and assessment of Swainson's hawks in Argentain following restrictions on monocrotophos use. *Ecotoxicology* **8**, 215–224.

Green RE and Balmford A (2005) A framework for improved monitoring of biodiversity: responses to the World Summit on Sustainable Development. *Conservation Biology* **19**, 56–65.

Hildrew A (2004) *FBA News* **25**.

Jones MB, Schildhauer MP, Reichman OJ and Bowers S (2006) The new bioinformatics: integrating ecological data from the gene to the biosphere. *Annual Review of Ecology, Evolution and Systematics* **37**, 519–544.

Krebs CJ (1991) The experimental paradigm and long-term population studies. *Ibis* **133**, 2–8.

Lamb EG, Bayne E, Holloway G, Schieck J, Soutin S, Herbers J and Haughland DL (2009) Indices for monitoring biodiversity change: are some more effective than others. *Ecological Indicators* **9**, 432–444.

Likens GE (1991) Human-accelerated environmental change. *BioScience* **41**(3), 130.

Likens GE (1998) Limitations to intellectual progress in ecosystem science. In *Successes, Limitations and Frontiers in Ecosystem Science*. (Eds ML Pace and PM Groffman) pp. 247–271. Springer-Verlag, New York.

Likens GE (2001) Ecosystems: Energetics and Biogeochemistry. In *A New Century of Biology*. (Eds WJ Kress and GW Barrett) pp. 53–88. Smithsonian Institution Press, Washington D.C.

Lindenmayer DB and Burgman MA (2005) *Practical Conservation Biology*. CSIRO Publishing, Melbourne.

Lindenmayer DB and Likens GE (2009) Adaptive monitoring – a new paradigm for long-term research and monitoring. *Trends in Ecology and Evolution* **24**, 482–86.

Lindenmayer DB, Likens GE, Franklin JF and Muntz R (2009) Opportunity in the wake of natural 'disasters'. *Science* **324**, 463.

Louv R (2005) *Last Child in the Woods. Saving Our Children from Nature-Deficit Disorder*. Algonquin Books of Chapel Hill, Chapel Hill, North Carolina.

Lovett GM, Burns DA, Driscoll CT, Jenkins JC, Mitchell MJ, Rustad L, Shanley JB, Likens GE and Haeuber R (2007) Who needs environmental monitoring? *Frontiers in Ecology and the Environment* **5**, 253–260.

McAlpine CA, Lindenmayer DB, Eyre TJ and Phinn SR (2002) Landscape surrogates of forest fragmentation: synthesis of Australian Montreal Process case studies. *Pacific Conservation Biology* **8**, 108–120.

McDonald E, Gordon A, Wintle BA, Walker S, Grantham H, Carvalho S, Bottrill M, Joseph L, Ponce R, Stewart R and Possingham HP (2008) 'True' conservation progress. *Science* **323**, 43–44.

Nielsen SE, Bayne EM, Schieck J, Herbers J and Boutin S (2007) A new method to estimate species and biodiversity intactness using empirically derived reference conditions. *Biological Conservation* **137**, 403–414.

Noss R (1996) The naturalists are dying off. *Conservation Biology* **10**, 1–3.

O'Neill G (2008) Jump-starting environmental monitoring. *Ecos* **143**, 14–17.

Pavlik BM and Barbour MG (1988) Demographic monitoring of endemic sand dune plants, Eureka Valley, California. *Biological Conservation* **46**, 217–242.

Pergams OR and Zaradic PA (2008) Evidence for a fundamental and pervasive shift away from nature-based recreation. *Proceedings of the National Academy of Sciences* **105**, 2295–2300.

Shrader-Frechette KS and McCoy ED (1993) *Method in Ecology: Strategies for Conservation*. Cambridge University Press, Cambridge.

Silver S (2006) Gaming the impact factor. *Frontiers in Ecology and the Environment* **4**, 283.

State of the Environment Report (2001) Biodiversity. Commonwealth of Australia, Canberra.

Steffen W, Burbidge A, Hughes L, Lindenmayer DB, Musgrave W, Stafford-Smith M and Werner P (2009) *Australia's biodiversity and climate change* CSIRO Publishing, Melbourne

The Heinz Center (2008) The State of the Nation's Ecosystems 2008. The H. John Heinz III Center for Science, Economics and the Environment and Island Press, Washington, D.C.

United Nations Environment Program (UNEP) (1999) Global Environmental Outlook 2000. United Nations Environment Programme, Nairobi, Kenya.

Van Horne B and Wiens JA (1991) Forest bird habitat suitability models and the development of general habitat models. US Fish and Wildlife Service, Washington, DC.

Wentworth Group (2008) Accounting for nature. A model for building the national environmental accounts of Australia. Wentworth Group of Concerned Scientists, Sydney.

Zaradic PA and Pergams OR (2007) Videophilia: implications for childhood development and conservation. *The Journal of Developmental Processes* **2**, 130–144.

INDEX

DATE DUE

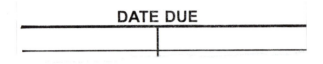